Sharpe's Story

THE STORY BEHIND THE SHARPE SERIES BY

Bernard Cornwell

First published in abbreviated form and as a limited
edition by HarperCollins Publishers, 2006.

This revised and expanded edition is published by
The Sharpe Appreciation Society, 2007.

THE SHARPE APPRECIATION SOCIETY

P. O. Box 14   P. O. Box 168
Lowdham   West Chatham
Notts, NG14 7HU   MA, 02669
United Kingdom   USA

www.southessex.co.uk

www.bernardcornwell.net

Printed and bound in Canada by Webcom
Design: GarryGatesDesigns

ISBN 13: 978-0-9722220-3-7

The sword on the back cover is an example of the 1796 pattern sword, carried throughout the war by Britain's heavy cavalry. The blade originally had a straight back edge, which unbalanced an already ill-weighted weapon, and troops who carried one into battle were permitted to make a leaf-point (as on this original weapon) by grinding down the backblade. Sharpe would carry nothing else.

The rifle is a replica, made for the Sharpe TV series, of the famous Baker Rifle which was issued to the Rifle Brigade in 1800 and stayed in service until the 1840's. It offered British skirmishers a considerable advantage over their French opponents who, thanks to Napoleon's prejudice against rifled weapons, were forced to carry smoothbore muskets.

INTRODUCTION

Sharpe's Story was first written for a bookstore-chain in Britain which wanted a pamphlet they could give away to customers who purchased *Sharpe's Fury*. As usual, the request came very late and the resulting booklet was written in a great hurry. This version is much longer. I am also including a much shorter essay, *Cakes and Ale*, because that explains some of the murkier wellsprings from which Sharpe emerged.

I am writing this on a chill summer's day on Cape Cod, but my life has been warmed and entertained by the arrival of a new Sharpe book. Well, an old Sharpe book, but in a new and astonishing disguise. It sits on my desk and I look at it with utter amazement: *L'Aigle de Sharpe*, it is called. *Sharpe's Eagle*, the very first Sharpe book, has just been published in France and I am gobsmacked. '*Découvrez Richard Sharpe, le meilleur ennemi de Napoléon*' it says on the back cover, which my lousy French would translate as 'Discover Richard Sharpe, Napoleon's worst enemy.' I doubt whether too many of the French want to make the discovery, but I'm flattered that so many other people have shown an interest in Sharpe over the years, and this booklet tries to answer some of the questions I'm frequently asked about the series. The most often asked question is whether there will be any more Sharpe books, and to discover the answer, read on.

Sharpe's Story

I'm often asked where Sharpe came from; whether I modelled him on some real person whose memoirs I had found, or whether his character is based on some friend of mine, but the truth is that he was inspired by neither. He came out of my dreams and I had lived with him for a very long time before he ever appeared on paper.

I first wrote about him when I was living in Belfast, though he was not called Sharpe then. It was 1978 and I gloried in the grand title of Head of Current Affairs Television for the BBC in Northern Ireland. I liked Belfast. In the late 1970's it was riven by sectarian violence, patrolled by soldiers and scarred by bombs, but it was also funny, intimate and friendly. I liked producing television too, but I had always wanted to be a novelist and, ever since finishing C.S. Forester's marvellous Hornblower novels, I had wanted to read a series of books which did for Wellington's army what Forester had done for Nelson's navy. I must have searched for that non-existent series for close to twenty years, and then, one wet winter's day in

Belfast, I decided to try and write it myself. I remember typing as the rain fell steadily beyond the window and the grey clouds hung low over that strangely beguiling city. As the poet wrote; 'Oh the bricks they will bleed and the rain it will weep, And the damp Lagan fog lull the city to sleep. It's to hell with the future, and live on the past, May the Lord in his mercy be kind to Belfast.' Belfast was certainly kind to me, but my hopes for being a novelist there went nowhere. That early attempt to write a novel of the Napoleonic Wars died almost as soon as I had begun it. The only memento of that first failed attempt is a handsome BBC notebook which I used to jot down my research, and which I still use.

But why did I so like stories of military history? It all went back to childhood. In 2005 the literary magazine *Granta* assembled an anthology of writers' experiences of adoption and, maybe stretching the definition of 'writer', asked me to contribute. My initial reaction was to say no, because my childhood experience was not happy, but then, before sending the refusal, I started typing. Writing *Cakes and Ale* took maybe ninety minutes and left me snarling, but I sent it to *Granta* anyway with the stipulation that the fee should go to charity. The piece has subsequently been published in the *New York Times* and in London's *Daily Telegraph*, and been translated into a dozen languages so the charity, I'm glad to say, did well from it. I've included the essay in this book, as an appendix, so I won't repeat much of it here, except to say that my adoptive parents belonged to a religious group called The Peculiar People (a 'sect of very ignorant people' according to Blunt's *Dictionary of Sects, Heresies, Ecclesiastical Parties and Schools of Religious Thought* - a verdict with which I would agree, though it does have an annoyingly patronising tone. On the other hand I can recommend Blunt's Dictionary as appropriate bathroom reading). The Peculiar People disapproved of many things, and among that list of forbidden fruit was military service and, in my reaction against their various prohibitions, I became fascinated by all things military (thank goodness they disapproved of wine, wild women and whoopee too). It was, I think, as simple as that. I became interested in military history because it was frowned on by the god-fearing people who adopted me.

The interest endured. By 1979, when I was 35, I still had the secret dream of writing a 'Hornblower-on-Land' series, but my first attempt had been a failure and I doubt I would have tried again except that in Edinburgh, while I was on a filming assignment, a blonde appeared in a hotel lobby. She was an American called Judy and Cupid's arrow struck me with the accuracy of a rifle bullet fired by Daniel Hagman. Judy, for all sorts of good reasons, could not move from the States to Northern Ireland, so I decided I would abandon television, give up Belfast and go to live in America instead. The trouble with that plan was that the US government refused me a work permit, so I airily promised Judy that I would earn a living as a writer.

Looking back I can see how daft it all was. I became, essentially, an illegal immigrant living in a tiny New Jersey apartment with a typewriter on a table made from a sheet of plywood propped up on breeze-blocks. The only thing I wanted to write was my Hornblower-on-Land series and so, with no other option if love was to flourish, I started again. This time, unlike my first effort in Belfast, things were more desperate. If Sharpe failed me or, more likely, if I failed Sharpe, then the course of true love would hit a massive roadblock. What little money I possessed would not last long, so speed was of the essence and *Sharpe's Eagle* was written in a hurry. I had never written a book before (my first failed attempt had stalled somewhere in the first chapter so doesn't count) and really had no clear idea how to go about it. Of course I knew I needed a hero, but I never once sat down and tried to delineate him in my mind; instead I let him develop as I wrote the book. I knew he would be a rifleman, because the rifle was unique to Wellington's troops and that would give him an edge over the enemy. I also knew he was an officer who had been promoted from the ranks, because that would give him some problems within his own army, and I knew he had once saved Wellington's life, which would be an advantage to him, but beyond that, Sharpe was pretty much a mystery to me when I started writing *Sharpe's Eagle*. I described him at the beginning of the book as tall and black-haired, which was fine till Sean Bean came along, after which I tried never to mention his hair colour again. I gave him a scarred cheek, though for the life of me I can never remember which cheek has the scar and I suspect it changes from book to book. What I did not give him was a name because I was looking for something as memorable and as quirky as Horatio Hornblower. Day after day passed as more pages piled up on my makeshift desk, and still he was called Lieutenant XXX. I made lists of names, none of which worked, and it began to annoy me, even began to hold up the writing, so I decided to replace XXX with a temporary name. I called my rifleman Richard Sharpe in homage to the great Cornwall and England rugby player, Richard Sharp, and I thought I would change it when the right name came along. But of course the new name stuck. Within a day or two I was thinking of him as Sharpe, and so he has remained.

Patrick Harper was easier to name. I had a friend in Belfast called Charlie Harper who had a son named Patrick. The problem was that the Harper family was not fond of the British, nor did they have cause to be, and I worried they would be offended if I named a soldier in Britain's army after their son. I asked their permission which was gladly given and so Harper has marched with Sharpe ever since.

The book was finished in about six months. I remember staring at the pile of paper and wondering what on earth I did next. Obviously I needed a publisher and, by chance, the person who had bought my London flat was a literary agent and so I sent the manuscript to him. His reply came more or less by return of post; 'no reader is interested in the British army'. True love seemed to be doomed, but by a stroke of good luck I met another London literary agent who was visiting New York, and within a week *Sharpe's Eagle* had a publisher and I had a contract to write six more books. A quarter century later I still have the same agent, the same publisher and the same wife, and in all that time I have never re-read *Sharpe's Eagle*. But not so long ago a reader told me his reaction to that first Sharpe book. "I thought it would be like every other book," he said, "but when Sharpe killed Berry I knew it was different. Other heroes would never have done that. They have scruples, but Sharpe doesn't." Ah! So right from the beginning Sharpe was a rogue. Berry was a fellow-British officer who managed to upset Sharpe, which is never a wise thing to do, and so one dark night Sharpe corners and subdues Berry.

Berry babbled again, pleaded, shook his head, dropped his sword and held his hands together as if in prayer to Sharpe. The Rifleman stared down. He remembered a strange phrase he had heard once at a church parade in far-off India. A chaplain had stood in his white surplice and out of the meaningless mumbles a phrase had somehow lodged in Sharpe's mind, a phrase from the Prayer Book that came back to him now as he wondered whether he really could kill a man for raping his woman. 'Deliver my soul from the sword, my darling from the power of the dog.' Sharpe had thought to let the man stand, pick up his sword and fight for his life. But he thought of the girl's terror, let the picture of her blood on the sheets feed his anger and then, as if he were tired and simply wanted to rest, he leaned forward with both hands on the hilt of his sword.

The babbling almost became a

scream, the body thrashed once, the blade went through skin and muscle and fat into Berry's throat and the lieutenant died.

There is lots that is familiar there, though if I were writing that episode now I would never have Sharpe wondering whether to kill a man who had raped his woman. He would have no hesitation at all these days. But Sharpe already displays the anger that fuels so much of his life. It is the anger of an unhappy childhood and of a man who has been forced to fight for every advantage that others were given, and that rage drives Sharpe. That internal anger also makes him very different from Hornblower who is so fair-minded and honourable. Sharpe is a rogue, and a dangerous one, but he is a rogue on our side. I note too that religion appears in the passage, which doesn't surprise me. I was immersed in the filth of religion through all my childhood and still have not succeeded in washing the stench away. Sharpe shares at least one characteristic with Hornblower, which is a dislike of parsons, so it is not surprising that he found the church parade 'meaningless mumbles.'

Sharpe's Eagle ended with Sir Arthur Wellesley saying, "Gentlemen, I give you *Sharpe's Eagle*." That started the tradition of ending each book with the two words of its title, though I had to make exceptions for Waterloo and Trafalgar . . . it would have been much too clumsy, almost as clumsy as the sword which Sharpe carried in the first book and, more or less, has carried ever since. "He could never carry that sword', an expert told me after *Sharpe's Eagle* was published in 1981. 'That sword' was the 1796 pattern Heavy Cavalry sword, a beast of a blade, ill-balanced and ineffective, but I liked the idea of Sharpe, a tall man, carrying such a butcher's weapon. He had, after all, to be distinctive, and so, despite being an officer, he carries his rifle still, and he also wants an effective sword. As a Rifle officer he is supposed to wear a light sabre, more as a badge of rank than as a weapon, but I knew Sharpe would want a blade capable of doing real damage. But had I got it all wrong in the first book? Had Sharpe, in truth, been stumbling around with an impossible blade getting tangled between his legs? Just then a friend in London wrote to say that a trooper's Heavy Cavalry sword was on sale in his local antique shop, and did I want it? I could not afford it, but decided I had to have it anyway, and when the blade reached New Jersey I slung the scabbard from a belt and wore it for a day or two and discovered, to my huge relief, that the expert was wrong. The antique dealer, in a covering letter, assured me the blade had been carried at Waterloo, and I like to think that is true. It certainly was used in action because the back-blade has been ground down to a point (the original sword was issued with an asymmetrical point which had the unhappy effect of glancing the blade off an enemy's ribs) and only troopers going into action were permitted to sharpen the blade's tip to a symmetrical point. The sword hangs now above the fireplace in my study. So Sharpe kept his heavy sword and carried it into his second adventure, *Sharpe's Gold*.

Sharpe lunged desperately for the eyes, but *El Catolico* just swayed to one side and his rapier came low at the Rifleman, aiming at the thigh to inflict another flesh wound and Sharpe had only one, desperate, insane idea left. He let the rapier come, kicked his right thigh forward and pushed *El Catolico's* blade painfully into his flesh to trap the sword . . . Sharpe put his own sword at *El Catolico's* throat, "a butcher's blade, eh?" he asked.

Reading that now, twenty six years after it was written, I suspect that the desperate insane idea belonged entirely to me. I had put Sharpe into a fight he could not win, and I had no idea how to get him out of it, and these days the idea of Sharpe trapping an opponent's sword by deliberately taking a flesh wound and thus risking gangrene or being permanently lamed strikes me as truly stupid. But I was still learning to be a novelist, and perhaps my naivety was disguised by the richness of the material I was describing in the novel.

Then the hill moved. The sound came, not through the air, but through the ground itself, like the groaning of rock, and the whole cathedral turned to dust, smoke and flames that were the colour of blood. Men could see things in the flames; great stones, timbers carried upwards as though they were feathers, and then the shock hit the French gunners like a giant, hot wind that came with the sound. It was like all the thunder of all the world poured into one town for one moment for one glimpse of the world's end.

The cathedral disappeared, turned into flame, and the castle was scythed clean from the ground, the stones tumbling like toy blocks. Houses were scoured into flaming shards. The blast took the north of the town, unroofed half the southern slope, and the bakery collapsed onto the ovens inside one of which Sharpe, deafened and gasping, choked on the thick dust. The girl gripped him, prayed for her soul and the blast went past like the breath of the Apocalypse.

That is a very shortened version of the destruction of Almeida. The town, a fortress guarding one of the roads into Portugal, still stands and visitors can walk the hugely impressive ramparts that surround it. At the top of the town, beside a graveyard dark with cypress trees, are the remains of the mediaeval castle which appear to have been scythed off at ground level. That scything was the result of the explosion on August 27th, 1810. The town, defended by a British and Portuguese garrison, had stored their ammunition in the crypt of the cathedral next door to the castle, and somehow, no one knows the exact cause, that makeshift magazine exploded. It was almost certainly an accident, probably caused by a leaking powder keg being carried out of the cathedral, and the resultant trickle served as a perfect train to carry the fire from an exploding French shell back down into the crypt. The explosion was a disaster for the British cause, dooming Almeida's garrison to surrender. The obvious plot would suggest that Sharpe must do everything he can to prevent the explosion, but right from the beginning of the book I knew that he would cause it. He would blow up Almeida despite the setback it would impose on Wellington's hopes, and despite the death and destruction it would cause. Sharpe was becoming less and less like Hornblower. He is proving ruthless and unscrupulous, but of course he will only cause disaster at Almeida because he knows the alternative is even worse.

Sharpe's Gold also began a lamentable tradition in the Sharpe books. The town communicated with the distant British lines by a telegraph system which had, originally, been developed by the Admiralty. Ships on blockade duty off the coast of France would be driven by a westerly gale to take refuge in Torbay and it was essential that this news be conveyed to London as fast as possible, and so a string of telegraphs ran from what is now Torquay to the Admiralty by what is now Trafalgar Square. A similar signalling system (which worked by running bladders up to the crosstrees of a mast) was established in Portugal and it was manned by naval personnel. In *Sharpe's Gold* the responsible officer at the Almeida station is a very young midshipman, I do not remember giving him a surname, but he was obviously a pleasant and enthusiastic youngster of about 15.

The cannon-ball, twenty four pounds of iron, struck only a glancing blow on one of the crosstrees. The telegraph was well made, jointed and bolted, but as the French ball spun off into the unknown the telegraph ripped itself from its base like a tree uprooted by a hurricane. The boy, holding onto a rope, was spun into the air, screaming until another halliard whiplashed round his neck and tore his head horribly from his shoulders. His blood sprayed the four men, and then the mast, still unbroken, pounded back onto the ramparts . . .

A young woman who worked for my publisher protested at this passage, saying it was too sad for such a promising young lad to die, and so, ever since, I have made a point of introducing such clean-cut youngsters into Sharpe's stories only to kill them off before the book's end. This went on until *Sharpe's Trafalgar*, where a nice young lad called Midshipman Collier died at Trafalgar, and when Judy, my wife, first encountered him (she reads every manuscript) she said she could not read on because she knew Collier would die. So, just to prove her wrong, I changed the ending and Collier lived, the only boy to survive a Sharpe story so far.

The destruction of Almeida was part of the 'war of the fortresses', the bloody sieges and battles that swirled around Elvas, Almeida, Ciudad Rodrigo and Badajoz. Those four strongholds guard the two main roads which lead from Spain into Portugal, and whoever holds those four vast citadels controls any war in the Iberian Peninsula. So long as the French held the fortresses (and

Almeida surrendered to them on the day after the explosion), so long could they continue their attempts to capture Portugal and thus force Wellington onto the defensive. If Wellington was to carry the war into Spain he had to capture the great strongholds, and the story of the siege of Badajoz in 1812 is one of the great tales of the war. It was the story I really wanted to tell in the first Sharpe book, but I reckoned I might not have the skills to do it as a first-time author, and so I had began Sharpe's tales in 1809. The story of Badajoz with all its horror and heroism comes in the third Sharpe book, *Sharpe's Company*. That book also introduces the malevolent Sergeant Obadiah Hakeswill. I have no idea where he came from. I was driving one day and the name simply popped into my head. Hakeswill. It's a marvellously villainous name, and he proved to be a terrific villain. A blue-eyed villain, I wrote:

Everything about Obadiah Hakeswill was graceless and repulsive to the point of fascination. His body was huge, but any man who mistook the belly for a sign of weakness would be caught by his arms and legs that had massive strength. He was clumsy, except when performing a drill movement, though even when he was marching there was a hint that, at any moment, he might become some snarling, shambling beast; half wild, half man. His skin was yellowish, a legacy of the Fever Islands. His hair was blond, going grey, and stretched thinly over his scarred scalp, falling lank to the stretched, tensed, obscenely mutilated neck.

Then along came the incomparable Pete Postlethwaite who played Obadiah in the Sharpe TV series, and I quite forgot that description. Ever since I have seen Hakeswill in my mind as he was portrayed by Pete Postlethwaite. It was a wonderful example of how an actor can improve a character. But why was Hakeswill's neck 'obscenely mutilated'? Because he had survived a judicial hanging. I remember writing that and pausing. Would anyone believe me? Was I stretching, not just Obadiah's neck, but credulity? I almost cut it out, thinking I would receive scornful letters, but somehow it seemed absolutely right for Obadiah to have been hanged and to have survived, and so I left it in. Then, months later, I discovered that so many folk survived judicial hangings that the Royal College of Surgeons published a by-law dealing with how such survivors were to be treated. The body of a hanged felon had value; first, presumably, to his (or her) family who might want to give the corpse a decent burial, and second to the men who made a living by selling dead bodies to surgeons who needed cadavers to perform anatomical research (for a wonderful discussion of this ghoulish trade I recommend Sara Wise's entrancing book, *The Italian Boy*). There was no proper police force at London's Tyburn (now Marble Arch), and there was often an unseemly scuffle as the two contending parties fought to cut down a hanged felon, and such was their haste that they sometimes cut the body down before it was dead (there was no 'long drop' in those days; instead you strangled slowly at the rope's end). If the body-snatchers won they would rush the hanged man to the nearest hospital, and often they were in too great a hurry because it was not uncommon for such 'corpses' to revive, and certainly a sufficient number survived to make the by-law necessary. If you did survive such an ordeal then you were not returned to the scaffold, but sent off to New South Wales, so, far from being unlikely, it seemed that Obadiah's history was almost commonplace, though Obadiah did avoid exile to Australia. Eventually, to avoid the rolling mauls that made Tyburn so unruly, the authorities moved the execution site to the Old Bailey, and the opening chapter of my novel, *Gallow's Thief*, offers a description of an execution in 1817. I imagine Sharpe, like any other Londoner, had often witnessed such executions. He grew up rough.

Sharpe's Company illustrates a truth of

historical fiction, that novelists must be story-
tellers before they are historians. The initial
horror of the assault on Badajoz was caused
by the failure of the British to get through
the breaches and the subsequent slaughter in
the ditches at the foot of those breaches. The
fortress fell because the fake attack, a feint on
the towering castle battlements designed solely
to draw defenders away from the breaches,
unexpectedly succeeded. But the drama of
the night, and there was much drama, was
concentrated on those terrible breaches where
so many men died, and that meant Sharpe had
to be in the thick of that awful assault, and
Sharpe is a hero and if he attacks a breach, he
gets through. So I changed history by making
Sharpe's assault on the breach successful. I
then confessed my sin in the Historical Note,
but I have no regrets at altering the truth. The
story is everything in a novel, and the story of
Badajoz is a soaring, ghastly tale.

I will die here, Sharpe thought,
at the foot of the breach, and then he
hated the bastards who would kill him
and the anger drove him up, stumbling
on the rubble, unable to fight, only to
climb, to carry the sword to French
flesh. There were men around him,
screaming unintelligibly, and the air
was thick with smoke, grapeshot and
flame. Harper was passing him, but

Sharpe, refusing to be second, drove towards the dark sky beyond the row of shining blades.

Private Cresacre was dying, his guts pooled blue in his lap, and Sergeant Read, the Methodist, the quiet man who never swore or drank, was blind and he could not cry because the guns had taken his eyes. And past the dying, mad with lust, a battle madness, went the dark horde who followed Sharpe and tore their hands on the rough stone, going up the slope, up, where they had never dreamed to go. You save your breath for climbing, but shouting dulls the fear, and who needs breath when death waits at the summit? A bullet clanged on Sharpe's sword, jerking it in his hand, but the blade was whole and the breach's top was near. He went to the right, his whole head ringing with a scream of death, and Harper's huge hand shoved him, heaved him, and Sharpe seized the thick chain which anchored the *chevaux de frise*. He was at the top, death's peak.

A *chevaux de frise* was a heavy log studded with blades and spikes, the Napoleonic version of razor wire. Badajoz's defenders were commanded by a resourceful and clever officer, General Philippon, and his devices ensured that no British soldier got through any of the breaches on that dreadful night, though thousands tried and hundreds died. The fall of the city was an accident, and that accident is an extraordinary story, but it was what happened after the city's capture that makes the story truly horrible. The sack of Badajoz by maddened British soldiers tarnished their victory 'as blood tarnished a sword', but it all made for a wonderful piece of fiction which was enlivened by Obadiah Hakeswill's vicious presence. Once inside Badajoz Hakeswill has managed to reach Sharpe's woman, Teresa, the mother of Sharpe's child, before Sharpe;

> "Hello, missy!" The face twitched, yellow in the candlelight, the mouth grinning, black teeth showing in rotten gums. "Hello! Remember me?"
>
> Lieutenant Knowles raised his sabre and the pistol flared, waking the baby as the bullet threw Knowles backwards through the door to fall with Hakeswill's cackle the last sound in his life.
>
> Hakeswill held the bayonet above the baby and pushed the pistol, still smoking, back into his jacket. He grinned at Teresa. "We didn't need

him," he said, nodding at Knowles's body, "only takes two to do what we're going to do. Just you and me, missy, just you and Obadiah!"

That's a shortened version, but copying and editing the episode reminds me of just how much I miss Obadiah. He was a perfect character to illustrate the horror of Badajoz's fall, which was, in itself, such a gift of a story to a novelist.

Another true story that lent itself to marvellous fiction was the battle of Salamanca which was one of Wellington's most complete victories and a masterpiece of opportunity and flair. That battle was the background for *Sharpe's Sword* in which Sharpe encounters one of my favourite heroines, La Marquesa de Casares el Grande y Melida Sadaba, a lady as beautiful as she is wicked. 'Other women, Sharpe guessed, would hate her, while men would follow her like lap dogs.' I received a plaintive letter after the book's publication, wondering why Sharpe had to meet women at all. The writer, it seemed, found Sharpe's rather frequent encounters with women as unwelcome interruptions to his military adventures and, while I really do my best to consider every reader's comment, I dismissed that one out of hand. Richard Sharpe has been very good to me over the years, so I try my hardest to reward him, and the Marquesa was one of my better presents to him. I also put him through the mill, and in *Sharpe's Sword* he is grievously wounded, which gave me the chance to describe a real character from the wars. He was an Irishman called Michael Connelley who would die, probably of alcoholic poisoning, soon after the battle of Salamanca. But during the campaign he was the orderly in charge of the 'death room', the place where horribly wounded soldiers were left to die as best they could. Salamanca's death room was in the basement of the Irish College, which still stands and, like everything else in that gorgeous city, is well worth a visit. A description of Connelley has survived, telling how he would encourage his dying boys to go well. He would tell them that there were French wounded in the room and that they must set an example of courage in front of the enemy, and I adapted that contemporary description for my own purposes:

It was cold in the death room. Connelley drank steadily. Some men breathed noisily, some moaned and some talked. Connelley prowled the central aisle from time to time, carrying a water bucket and a ladle, and he would feel the feet of the patients to see whether they had died. He came to Sharpe and crouched beside him. Sharpe's breathing was shallow, moaning slightly in his throat, and Connelley put a hand on the naked shoulder and found it was cold. "Ah, you poor man, you'll catch your death." He lumbered to the table, found a blanket that he shook as if to free the lice that infested its seams, then laid it over Sharpe. A man at the room's far end cried out in sudden pain. "Whoa there, lad," Connelley called, "whoa! Gentle now! Die well, die well!" A Frenchman cried and Connelley squatted beside him and talked of Ireland. He told the uncomprehending Frenchman of Connaught's beauty, of its women, of fields so fat that a lamb was full grown in a week, of rivers so thick with fish that the trout begged to be caught, and the Frenchman quieted and Connelley patted his hair and told him he was brave.

Connelley's funeral offered a glimpse of the army's rough humour. One of the pall-bearers had a great ability to mimic the dead man's voice and used it to call for help. The procession, which was well-attended, stopped as the coffin lid was prised up, at which point the deception was revealed to great merriment. One of the things that annoys me is historical novels that contain no humour, as if our ancestors never laughed. Men (especially men) use humour to confront danger, embarrassment or almost any uncomfortable situation, and a novel without humour, to me, is a novel that does not convince.   I n most respects the humour does not change, though I'm not sure how funny we would find a practical joke which I discovered in John Shipp's memoirs. His battalion was on board a transport ship, going to India, and it was thought a fine jest that the steep companionway ladders were greased with soap to break unwary mens' legs.

Some characters, like Connelley, come fully-formed from the records of the war, others simply spring from nowhere and take over a book. That happened in *Sharpe's Enemy*. I needed a senior officer to give Sharpe some orders, then decently fade away, and so I invented a convenient Scottish general called Nairn and I assumed he would do his duty and then vanish from the book, but Nairn simply refused to leave the story.

"I'm a harmless old man, Sharpe," Nairn said, "left in charge of this madhouse while the Peer gallivants round half the bloody Peninsula. I am supposed, God help me, to be running this Headquarters. Me! If I had time, Sharpe, I suppose I could lead a winter campaign. I could inscribe my name in glory, but I don't have bloody time. Look at this." He picked a paper from the pile beside him. "A letter, Sharpe, from the Chaplain-General. The Chaplain-General, no less! He is in receipt of a salary of five hundred and sixty five pounds a year, Sharpe, and in addition is named advisor on the establishment of semaphore stations for which nonsensical bloody job he receives a further six hundred pounds! And what does God's vicar to His Majesty's army do with his well paid time? He writes to me thus. 'I require of you to report on the containment of Methodism within the army.' Good God, Sharpe, what's a man to do with such a letter?"

"I wouldn't know, sir."

"I would. That's why I'm a Major-General." Nairn threw the letter onto the fire.

Nairn was a happy invention. Less happy was my decision to kill Obadiah Hakeswill at the end of *Sharpe's Enemy*, a choice I have regretted ever since. Truly good villains are hard to come by, and I threw Obadiah away. There would be a chance to resurrect him in the Indian novels, but how I have wished for Obadiah in other books! I am often asked who my favourite character is from all my books, and I very often answer with Obadiah's name. He might be vile, but he does light up every page on which he appears! I am tempted sometimes to invent an identical twin for him, Jedediah Hakeswill, but that seems a little too obvious. Some readers were also upset that Teresa died in *Sharpe's Enemy*. She was Sharpe's first true love, but he was not really ready to settle down and Teresa had to go. What happened to their daughter? I get letters almost every week asking that and one day, no doubt, I shall find out the answer.

Sharpe's Honour provided the opportunity for another splendid set-piece taken straight from history. That was the sack of the French baggage train after the battle of Vitoria. The French, retreating from Spain, were taking all their plunder with them, and they lost it along with the battle. Many British soldiers became wealthy that day.

Sharpe's horse trampled on leather-bound books, books that had been made before the printing press had been invented, books made by patient men over months of work. A tapestry that had been woven in Flanders when Queen Elizabeth was a child was torn by two women to make blankets. Another woman, bottle in hand, danced between the abandoned wagons with the gilded coat of a Royal Chamberlain on her shoulders. She wore nothing else. A soldier, drunk on brandy, plucked the coat away and she hit him with her bottle. Silver Spanish dollars, each worth five English shillings, were strewn in the mud like pebbles. No one wanted silver when there was so much gold.

Muleteers were using paintings by Rubens as tarpaulins. The Spanish crown jewels disappeared that day and have never been recovered. Wellington, of course, was furious, and it was after the sack that he called his soldiers, 'the scum of the earth'. That phrase has stuck to Wellington and is often used to portray him as an aristocratic snob. Well, he was a snob, but he took care of his men and, in truth, paid them many a compliment. He was intensely proud of his army, but he was also aware of the common soldier's propensity to get stinking drunk. He had been relying on the French baggage-train to supply him with the money to pay the army (and a host of other debts that the British had incurred), and the loss of it was a severe blow and it showed in his angry response. Nevertheless that scathing verdict was one that Sharpe would doubtless have agreed with, but he was one of the scum and proud of it.

An 'alley-cat', Lady Camoynes calls Sharpe in *Sharpe's Regiment*, and so he is, but a cat with very sharp claws. I took him away from the war in that book and sent him back to Britain where he has to discover the missing second battalion of his regiment. It was a chance to describe how recruits were encouraged to join the ranks, and Sharpe, by pretending to be one of those volunteers, uncovers the greed of Lord Fenner and Sir Henry Simmerson. He also, fatefully, gets entangled with Jane Gibbons, sister of an old enemy, thus proving that Sharpe, excellent soldier though he may be, is often a fool with women, though in his next adventure, *Sharpe's Siege*, he makes the connection that will lead him to Lucille, the woman with whom he will eventually settle. The connection is through Lucille's brother, Henri Lassan, who commands the fort at Arcachon. *Sharpe's Siege* is one of the few books in the series where the action is entirely fictional, and it remains one of my favourites. I am not sure why. Poor Major Hogan, who has been Sharpe's patron since the very first novel, dies in the book, and I cannot now remember why I thought his time had come, but I do try to kill off characters unexpectedly, as much as anything to keep readers slightly off balance. A happier note is supplied by the presence of William Frederickson who made his first appearance in *Sharpe's Enemy*, and who will stay with Sharpe for much of the rest of the series.

> Captain Frederickson looked villainous. His left eye was gone, its socket covered by a black patch that was green at the edges. Most of his right ear was missing and two of his front teeth were clumsy fakes. The wounds had all been taken on the battlefield.

That is 'Sweet William', whose creation occurred just after Judy and I were married. A young Baptist minister, the Reverend William Frederickson, conducted the ceremony, and he decided to read a Sharpe book before he spliced us. He told me he enjoyed the book, but ventured the criticism that Sharpe was a dangerously violent man. The Reverend William, on the other hand, is a shining example of the Christian virtues, being gentle, decent, peaceable and kind, but his reservations about Sharpe persuaded me to create a character even more savage than Sharpe and to call him William Frederickson. The Reverend has long forgiven me and is, I think, secretly proud of his namesake. *Sharpe's Siege* also features the wily Pierre Ducos, the French intelligence agent who proves a determined and clever opponent, and General Calvet, my favourite Frenchman in the Sharpe books. His wife sleeps on a pillow stuffed with the hair of Cossacks killed by Calvet's men during the retreat from Moscow, while Calvet himself likes to boast of having eaten roast buttock of corporal, well-peppered, during that campaign. In time Calvet and Sharpe will meet properly and like each other.

I am frequently asked when Sharpe is going to take part in the War of 1812. Most of those letters come from Canadians, rightly proud of the repulse of the American invasions of Canada. Riflemen did serve in that mostly pointless war, but Sharpe will never get to fight there and the reason why is in *Sharpe's Siege*. My only regret about the promise he makes (and keeps) not to fight against the USA is that he thereby missed out on the burning of Washington DC, an episode Sharpe would have thoroughly enjoyed, but on the other hand he would have hated the Battle of New Orleans, so one way and another he's better off staying on the eastern side of the Atlantic where, after the fictional siege of Arcachon, he takes part in the real battle of Toulouse. This is *Sharpe's Revenge*, which takes Sharpe out of the wars and into peacetime. It tells the tale of the killing of Pierre Ducos, and allies Sharpe with General Calvet. It does much more, though. It brings Lucille into his life.

Sharpe turned and pushed Frederickson out of the kitchen. He had seen the slim, black-dressed woman turn back from the vats. And in her hands now was a great brass-muzzled horse pistol. Her grey eyes held nothing but bitter hatred and Sharpe knew, with the certainty of the doomed, that everything had gone wrong. He pushed Frederickson desperately into the yard and he tried to throw himself out of the door, but he knew he was too late. His body flinched from the terrible pain to come. He had already begun to scream in anticipation when Lucille Castineau pulled the trigger and Sharpe's world turned to thunder and agony. He felt the bullets strike him like massive blows, and he saw a sear of flame flash its light above him, and then, blessedly, as the gun's stunning echo died away, there was just nothing.

That's the way to meet the woman with whom you will spend the rest of your life! Sharpe will, indeed, settle in France with Lucille, and of all the things he has ever done, that has surprised me the most. I knew his marriage to Jane Gibbons was on the rocks, but I assumed he would find himself some other woman and settle down to a life in the English countryside. Lucille was intended for Frederickson, indeed I had deliberately introduced her into *Sharpe's Revenge* as a reward for him. He had endured a lot for Sharpe over the last few books and he had never been fortunate in love, so I thought Lucille Castineau would be a perfect consolation. Then, perversely, Sharpe fell in love with her. I tried to prevent it, but when a character takes off on their own like that, there's very little a writer can do, and so Sharpe and Lucille fall into each other's arms, and poor Frederickson is both offended and jilted. The French actress Cecile Paoli played Lucille in the Sharpe TV series, and I thought she was perfect; exactly as I saw Lucille in my imagination.

By now the Sharpe series had reached 1814 and I thought his long story was drawing to a close. Sharpe had no idea, of course, that Waterloo was still to be fought, and at the end of *Sharpe's Revenge* he rides into the sunset thinking that his fighting days are over.

He clicked his tongue and urged the horse into a trot. He felt dazed. There was no more war, no more soldiers, no more fear. No more Emperor, no more Harper, no more gunsmoke skeined above a field of blood. No more closing of ranks, no more miles of pain, no more skirmish chain. No more cavalry in the dawn and no more picquets in the dusk. There was only Lucille and what Sharpe thought was a love sufficient for both their lives. He rode on into France, his back turned on all he had fought for, for now it was all gone; the wars, a friendship and an enemy, all gone in Sharpe's revenge.

He was wrong about no more fighting, but right about Lucille. They do stay together, right to their end, whenever that is. I am often asked whether I will kill Sharpe off in a book. No! No way! In my mind Sharpe and Lucille fade away into a happy old age and, I hope, die simultaneously in their own bed. The TV film *Sharpe's Challenge* seemed to imply that there was no more Lucille and some readers were worried by this and wrote to me. I assure them that what is in the books is the Authorised Version, and what the films do to make their plots work is apocryphal. I do not mind that, but nor do I feel committed to their version over mine. Sharpe and Lucille live happily ever after, or at least into old age. There is a glimpse of them in Normandy just after the wars in *Sharpe's Ransom*, one of the three short stories that are available from the Sharpe Appreciation Society (www.southessex. co.uk). Sharpe is no longer a soldier. He's a farmer, scratching to make ends meet.

Richard Sharpe tugged off his boots, put both hands in the small of his back, arched his spine and grunted with pain. "I hate bloody cogwheels," he said.

"What is wrong with the bloody cogwheels?" Lucille asked.

"Rusted solid," Sharpe said as he tipped a cat off a kitchen chair. "Sluice gates won't work till the rust is cleared and no one's greased those wheels in years." He groaned as he sat down. "I'll have to chip the things down to bare metal, then clear the leat."

"The leat?" Lucille asked. She was still learning English.

"The channel that takes the water to the mill, love. It's full of rubbish."

Sharpe poured himself some wine. "It'll take me a week to clear that."

"It's Christmas in two days," said Lucille.

"So?"

"So at Christmas you rest." Lucille declared, "and the leat and the sluice gate and the bloody cogwheels can all rest. It is a holiday! I shall cook you a goose."

"You cooked my goose long ago, girl," Sharpe said.

The only shooting Sharpe does in Normandy is to kill the foxes that eat his lambs. His world has contracted to a farm, a woman and his children. It astonished me that Sharpe went to live in France, yet now it seems the only possible course open to him. Sharpe was always an outsider and he could never have been content in Britain after the war. But as a British soldier living among the erstwhile enemy he is as happy as when he was a man from the ranks surviving in the officer's mess. He likes being the square peg. And he loves Lucille. Lucky Sharpe.

Then came the Emperor's escape from Elba and the extraordinary story of Waterloo. I remember struggling with *Sharpe's Waterloo* which, for obscure reasons, was published as, simply, *Waterloo*, in the US. Most historical novels contain two stories; the big story and the little story. Think of *Gone With the Wind*. The big story is the American Civil War and who will win it, while the small story is whether Scarlett can save Tara. The trick of it is to put the small story in the foreground and the big story in the background, but in *Sharpe's Waterloo* that proved impossible. There really is no small story in the book, just the huge, magnificent, appalling and sprawling story of Waterloo itself. I spent weeks working on a plot that revolved about Jane, Sharpe's estranged wife, and her lover, Lord Rossendale, and a vestige of that tale lingers somewhere deep in the book, but in truth that story never worked. I tried and tried, then one day just got fed up with trying and instead went straight into the tale of the campaign.

It was dawn on the northern frontier of France; a border marked only by a shallow stream which ran between the stunted trunks of pollarded willows. A paved road forded the stream. . . . . It was a perfect midsummer's dawn on the northern border of France and for a moment, for a last heart-aching moment, the world was at peace.

That was dawn on the 15th of June, and between that moment and sunset on the 18th the British were to be involved in two battles, Quatre Bras and Waterloo itself. The book tells the tale of those fights, and how Napoleon very nearly managed to split the allied armies (British and Prussian) and then defeat them one by one. The drama of the campaign is such that no small story can live beside it. Not just the drama of the day itself when, till the very last moment, it seemed the

French must win, but the human drama of the two greatest soldiers of the age at last meeting on a battlefield.

No one would dispute Napoleon's place in the pantheon of great military leaders, but Wellington, to my mind, is a much greater battlefield general. Wellington, of course, was never a 'war leader' like Napoleon. He did not play dice with nations. He operated at a more modest level, as the leader of an army, and it is remarkable that, unlike the Emperor, he never suffered a battlefield defeat. He had a great talent for soldiering, a clear eye, a decisive mind, and a comprehensive grasp of what his men were capable of doing. His men liked him. They did not love him as the French soldiers loved Napoleon, but the Emperor was a politician who knew how to tweak mens' affections. In return they worshipped him. But Wellington? He did not want to be worshipped. He had, he said, no small talk. He did not know how to talk to common soldiers and was embarrassed when he had to. He was a snob. Yet his men liked him because they knew he did not risk their lives unnecessarily. In battle he protected them, usually by placing them on a reverse slope where they were out of sight of the enemy, and the soldiers in his army knew that he did not throw away their lives lightly. After Austerlitz a French general lamented the vast number of French dead on the battlefield and received a scornful look from Napoleon. "The women of Paris," the Emperor said, "can replace those men in one night." Wellington would never have said that. It was only in sieges that he lost his ability to keep casualties to a minimum, but he was never at his best besieging fortresses. He was once asked what was the greatest compliment he had ever received, and he told how he had visited the wounded after the battle of Albuera. That was a dreadful battle in which the British were commanded by General Beresford and it nearly ended in disaster. British casualties were horribly high. "The enemy," the French commander said, "was beaten, but did not know it." The battle was won, but at an awful price and two days later Wellington visited the wounded. As usual he was embarrassed when he had to speak to the common soldiery. He came to a large room in a convent where scores of redcoats were lying in pain. He claimed he did not know what to say, so cleared his throat and, rather lamely, said that he was sorry to see so many of them there. "My lord," a corporal spoke up from among the injured, "if you had been at the battle then not so many of us would be here." It was, indeed, a great compliment.

Behind almost all the Sharpe books is the relationship between Wellington and Sharpe. They are not men who would instinctively

like each other. The Duke, as he became, is
cold and taciturn. He did not approve of men
like Sharpe. He did not like seeing officers
promoted from the ranks; "they always take
to drink," he said dismissively. Sharpe, on the
other hand, is scornful of men like Wellington
who were born with the privileges of rank,
money and connections. Sharpe cannot buy
his way up the army's ladder, yet that is how
Wellington gained his first promotions. Yet
the two men are inextricably tied because
Sharpe once saved Wellington's life. The
general is aware that he ought to be grateful,
and he is, in a grudging way, while Sharpe,
who ought to dislike the general, admires him
instead. He knows a good soldier when he
sees one. Birth and privilege have nothing to
do with it, efficiency is all. They will never
be friends, they will always be distant, but
they need each other. They even, I think,
like each other, but neither knows how to
bridge the gap to express that liking. And
Sharpe is always doing over-dramatic things,
of which the Duke disapproves. Wellington
liked steady unflashy officers, who quietly did
their duty, and he was quite right to approve
of such good men. Sharpe is anything but
quietly dutiful. One of my favourite moments
in *Sharpe's Waterloo* is when he arrives at the
Duchess of Richmond's ball on the eve of the
battle.

Silence spread slowly across the supper tables as the hundreds of guests turned to stare at the Rifleman who, in turn, searched the tables for the Duke. A woman gasped because Sharpe was drenched in blood. His face was powder stained and his uniform darkened with gore. Every other man in the room wore white breeches and silk stockings, yet here, like the ghost in Macbeth, came a soldier as bloodied and grim-faced as slaughter.

Which more or less sums up Sharpe. The odd man out, but a very useful man on the battlefield.

Sharpe's horse was wounded. It screamed with pain as he crashed a musket aside with his sword then lunged at a Frenchman's face. The man recoiled then went down beneath the bayonets of two snarling redcoats. The enemy were edging back. The column was so tightly packed that the French had no room to use their weapons properly. Sharpe's men were keening as they killed, crooning a foul music as they lunged and stabbed and gouged and fought across the dead. Sharpe's horse half stumbled on a corpse and he flailed with the sword to keep his balance. The ridge stank of blood and sweat and powder smoke. A vast crash announced that Harper had fired his volley gun point blank into the ranks of the Guard, and now the Irishman threw himself into the space his bullets had made. He widened the space with his sword-bayonet. Each thrust accompanied by a Gaelic war-cry. Ahead of Sharpe an Eagle swayed over the bearskin ranks. He cut his sword towards it, but the French were so closely packed that he could not force a path towards the trophy. He swore at a man as he killed him, then drove the sword into a moustached, sun-tanned face and twisted the steel to flense the man's cheek away.

That is the battle's end, the defeat of the Imperial Guard that provoked the French panic and flight. And so the fighting ends and next dawn Sharpe wakes amidst the remnants of carnage.

Sharpe was staring beyond the battlefield to where the new sunlight glowed on trees unmarked by fire and where the air smelt summer sweet. The cloudless sky promised a day for haymaking, or a day for lovers to stroll through heavy-leafed woods to rest beside the green cool of a stream bank. It was a midsummer's day on the border of France, and the world was at peace.

And that, I thought, was that. The end of the Sharpe series. I had written eleven novels, the same number as in Forester's Hornblower series, and I had taken Sharpe from Talavera to Waterloo, and now his world was at peace. Sharpe could go back to Normandy and to Lucille, while I would try my hand at other books. Sharpe was finished.

*   *   *

Then things grew complicated. Actually they had grown complicated a couple of years before I wrote *Sharpe's Waterloo* when a TV production company had announced that they wanted to make a series of films about Sharpe. I was, of course, delighted even though I did not believe that any such films would ever be made. The problem which the producers faced was the usual one, money. The budget for a Sharpe TV film is immense, and there never is enough money, and raising it is a huge challenge, but there was a chance that a Spanish production company would invest in the project. What the producers needed, therefore, was a new story set at the beginning of Sharpe's career which would include a Spanish hero. I still did not think the project would get anywhere, but it was foolish to ignore the chance that it might, so I wrote *Sharpe's Rifles* with Blas Vivar as the Spaniard who could provoke the desired cheque. Vivar meets Sharpe while Sharpe is fighting Harper, one of the best fight scenes in any of the Sharpe books.

> Harper would not back down. He punched back and drew blood from Sharpe's nose and lips, then drove him reeling backwards. Sharpe slipped on snow, tripped on the floor's rubble and fell. He saw the massive boot coming and twisted clear. He came up from the floor, snarling through blood, and grabbed Harper's crossbelt. The Irishman was himself off balance now and Sharpe turned him, swung him, then let go. Harper spun away, staggered and fell hard against the wall. A stone gouged blood down his left cheek.

And so it goes on, for more than three pages, until Vivar stops it. Sharpe and Harper become friends, of course. The book was published and I heard no more about any TV series, and I went on to write *Sharpe's Revenge* and *Sharpe's Waterloo*, and decided that the proposed films had been a flash in the pan. A flash in the pan is when a musket flint fires the priming powder in the lock, but doesn't set off the main charge in the barrel, and *Sharpe's Rifles* had all the feel of a misfired book. It had been a gamble, it had been written out of sequence, and I rather regretted the time I had spent on it. I liked it, but did not like writing out of chronological order. Sharpe, as far as I was concerned, had finally hung up his boots.

I could not have been more wrong. Soon after *Sharpe's Waterloo* was published I heard that the TV series was going to be made after all. And suddenly, to my astonishment, it was being made. A film crew was in the Ukraine, actors were there, and it was all real. Then, just as suddenly, it was all over. The actor playing Sharpe had a dreadful accident while playing football against the Ukrainian extras, and he was not going to be able to walk for six months, and the whole project seemed doomed. Somehow the producers rescued it, but they now needed a new actor to play Sharpe, and they needed him on very short notice. There was no time to do auditions, and the only actor available was Sean Bean who unexpectedly found himself on a plane to Simferopol (known to all the film crew as Simply-Awful).

How lucky can a man be? Me, I mean. To have Sean Bean step into Sharpe's boots at such short notice and then prove to be the quintessential Sharpe? Sean was a revelation.

For a start, of course, he's a terrific actor, but in many ways his own character is not unlike Sharpe's. There is toughness and anger in Sean, and a wariness of folk he does not know well. He is, like Sharpe, a formidable man. Folk instinctively treat him with respect, but then, suddenly, the smile will break and you see the core decency. The greatest compliment I can pay Sean, other than saying that I like him hugely, is that he really did take over Sharpe. I hear Sean's voice when I write Sharpe. It is a wonderful coincidence of actor and character, and I hope Sean feels the same. In the last couple of years I've been asked frequently whether it is true that I disapproved of Sean being cast as Sharpe. Somehow, I have no idea how, a newspaper printed that I had opposed the choice, but that was never true. From the start I knew Sean was the right man, and that opinion has only grown stronger. Then there was Daragh O'Malley, who played Harper, and that was another marvellous coincidence. Harper is easy-going compared to Sharpe (who is strung tighter than a war-drum) and Daragh throws a wry, accepting, tolerant gaze on the world's idiocies. Talking with Daragh you get the impression that he sees all, understands all and forgives all (Sharpe sees all, understands all and then thumps it). Daragh O'Malley also brings an extraordinarily sharp mind to his acting. He is a good man, and he and Sean play well off each other.

So, to my utter astonishment, there was going to be a TV series after all. By now I had abandoned any hope of seeing it and had started the Starbuck books, the tale of a young northerner who finds himself fighting for the Confederacy in the American Civil War. I was enjoying those books, not least because Sharpe's son appears in them. You are never told that Patrick Lassan is Sharpe's son, but the clues are all there. He is a Frenchman with an English father and he carries his father's sword, which is a British 1796 pattern heavy cavalry blade. Then it became clear that Sean Bean and Daragh O'Malley would be on the television playing Sharpe and Harper and it became obvious that I should go back to writing Sharpe. Which is why Nathaniel Starbuck has enjoyed such a long rest ever since. It was the TV series that really provoked the new Sharpe books. That decision was entirely venal. If a Sharpe TV series is being shown then it helps to have new Sharpe books in the shops, so back to Sharpe I went.

The first of the new books was *Sharpe's Devil*. I had been reading a biography of Lord Cochrane, the madcap Scottish admiral who was as much his own enemy as he was a scourge of the French, and I came across a strange story of his attempt to rescue Napoleon from St Helena (the idea was that

Napoleon would become Emperor of South America; weird but true). It intrigued me. *Sharpe's Devil* was supposed to be about that rescue attempt, but somehow the plot never jelled, and I confess this is my least favourite Sharpe story. It has its moments though, and one of my favourites is when Donna Louisa Vivar (an old friend) seeks Sharpe out in his Normandy farmhouse. Sharpe, not expecting visitors, is ready to turn her carriage away. I describe his face as 'sour and unwelcoming', and somehow that sums him up. My other favourite moment in *Sharpe's Devil* is when Sharpe meets Napoleon in Longwood House on Saint Helena.

It was all so utterly different from everything Sharpe had anticipated. Later, trying to reconcile reality with expectation, Sharpe wondered just what he had thought to find inside the yellow-walled house. An ogre? A small toad-like man with smoke coming from his nostrils? A horned devil with bloody claws? But instead, standing on a hearth rug in front of an empty fireplace, Sharpe saw a short, stout man wearing a plain green riding-coat with a velvet collar, black knee breeches and coarse white stockings. In the velvet lapel of the coat was a miniature medallion of the *Légion d'Honneur.*

All those details Sharpe noticed later, as the interview progressed, but his first impression as he went through the door was the shock of familiarity. This was the most famous face in the world, a face repeated on a million pictures, a million etchings, a million plates, a million coins. This was a face so familiar to Sharpe that it was truly astonishing to see it in reality . . . . . Bonaparte was fatter than Sharpe had expected. He was unhealthily bloated like a dead beast swollen with noxious vapours. His face was sallow and his fine hair was lank. Sweat pricked at his forehead. His nose was thin and straight, his chin dimpled, his mouth firm and eyes extraordinary.

I had to invent the details of Longwood because, though I try to visit everywhere that Sharpe goes, Saint Helena was a terrible long way off, and few boats go there, and even if you do reach the island there will be no chance of landing if the wind is blowing too hard from the wrong direction or if the sea is too lumpy. So I never tried to get there and, instead, drew the details of the house from various books. Years later I was lucky enough to reach Saint Helena and discovered, to my relief, that my picture was accurate. The one thing which struck me at Longwood, and which I have never seen remarked on in any book about the Emperor, is how small the rooms were. Napoleon was a man who loved palatial living. Wellington did not care about the size of his headquarter's accommodation and often chose fairly humble houses, but the Emperor had a predilection for soaring ceilings, sweeping staircases and grand rooms. In Longwood he must have felt cramped. The only largish room is the front room which has his billiard table, but the rest are low-ceilinged and tiny. And the Atlantic fog would have wrapped about the windows for months on end. He must have hated Longwood.

Sharpe, unlike the Emperor, survived Saint Helena. Then Muir Sutherland and Michael Craddock, the Sharpe TV producers, asked for another story. Their reason escapes me now, but there must have been a good one because I wrote *Sharpe's Battle* for them. I could not write it in time for the script-writer who only saw the first half of the book, so the second half of the TV story is utterly different. *Sharpe's Battle* was slotted into the centre of the existing books and told the tale of Fuentes d'Onoro, a battle on the Portuguese border. Curiously the battle is recorded on the Arc de Triomphe in Paris as a French victory, which it decidedly was not, but I suppose the poor darlings have to put up a few defeats to make the arch look impressive. Fuentes d'Onoro was a desperate battle that, unusually, lasted more than a day, and its climax came in hand-to-hand fighting in the cramped alleyways of the village and around the small graveyard above the houses.

The front men fell, but those behind leaped over their dying comrades to assault the graveyard wall. Bayonets and musket stocks slashed over the stones, then the French grenadiers surged across the wall, even pushing it down in places to begin hunting the survivors up through the heaped graves and fallen stones and shattered wooden crosses. More Frenchmen came from the village to bolster the attack, then a splintering deluge of rifle and musket fire flashed from the stony outcrops just above the blood-greased slope. Grenadiers fell and rolled downhill. A second British volley whipped over the gun-churned graves as still more redcoats arrived to line the ridge's crest and fire their rolling volleys from beside the church and from the saddle of grassland where Wellington had watched aghast as this spring French tide had risen almost to his horse's hooves.

The tide recedes, but comes again. The French kept trying to break through the village and Wellington kept feeding reinforcements into the struggle. It was alley-fighting, gutter-fighting, the kind Sharpe was made for.

"Fire!" Sharpe shouted and the volley whipped over the dead grenadiers as Sharpe's men charged out of the smoke and struggled over the warm heap of bloody dead. The French ahead were desperately reloading, but their fixed bayonets impeded their ramrods and they were still trying to load when Sharpe's charge smashed home and the killing began again. Sharpe's sword arm was weary, his throat was hoarse from shouting and his eyes were stinging from powder smoke, sweat and blood, but there could be no rest. He rammed the sword home, twisted it, pulled it out, then rammed it forward again. A Frenchman aimed his musket at Sharpe, pulled the trigger and was rewarded with a hangfire as the powder in the pan exploded, but did not set off the charge in the barrel. The man screamed as the sword stabbed home. Sharpe was so tired from the killing that he was holding the big sword with both hands, his right hand on the hilt and his left gripping the lowest part of the blade so that he could shove it hard into the press of men. The crush of bodies was so great that there were times when he could hardly move and so he would claw at the faces nearest him, kick and bite and butt with his head until the French moved or fell or died and he could climb over another body and snarl forward with the bloody sword dripping.

The awful alleys where Sharpe fought are still there, or some of them, for much of the village is abandoned. Twenty-five years ago, when I first visited Fuentes d'Onoro, I struggled through thorns to a dilapidated house and found, in its rotting doorpost, the rusted tip of a bayonet. It's surprising that such relics are still there after two hundred years. The major battlefields have been swept by metal detectors searching for musket balls, but even so, walking along a path beneath Burgos Castle, I once picked up two balls within five paces, and at Fort Napoleon I found three canister balls in the grass. The battlefields of India yield dozens of such things; you only have to kick a furrow at Assaye to find the bullets.

And it was to India that Sharpe would go next.

*　　*　　*

India had always been a part of Sharpe's 'back-story'. Even in the very first book, *Sharpe's Eagle*, India is mentioned. It helped explain much about Sharpe; how he had learned to read and, crucially, how he had saved Wellington's life and was thus rewarded with a commission. So India was useful to me, but I never had any intention of telling the Indian stories. I knew very little about India, and sources for the Indian campaigns of Sir Arthur Wellesley (as Wellington was then called) were very skimpy compared with the vast amount written about his Peninsular and Waterloo campaigns. I also had a conviction that I could not write convincingly about any battle unless I had visited the place, and I had never been to India and, because I really dislike hot weather, I had no particular wish to go.

But the TV series was now stretching into its third season and I was receiving letters asking for more Sharpe adventures, so it was time to bite the bullet and visit India. Judy and I were to make four trips altogether. My wife is a gentle soul; a yoga teacher, pacifist and vegetarian, but it has been her fate to wander the world exploring battlefields. She endures my enthusiasm patiently, but she enjoyed the

Indian trips more than the others, perhaps because India is the source of yoga. I was wary of going because I expected the battlefields to have changed beyond recognition, but in truth they are the least altered sites I have ever visited. Seringapatam, where *Sharpe's Tiger* is set, was a considerable town in 1799 when the British laid siege to it. I thought that by now the population explosion in India would have expanded the town into a small city, and that the walls would have been destroyed or hidden by development and that I would have to scratch around in back alleys to find even a remnant of the town Sharpe knew. In fact the town has shrunk to a village so that the impressive ramparts surround a great area of vacant land. It is a marvellous place.

Sharpe's Tiger was fun to write. It had two great villains. The first was the Tippoo Sultan whose reputation in Britain was that of a cruel tyrant. In fact he was an enlightened man who did much to improve the lives of his Mysorean subjects, but he fell foul of the expanding British interest. He could be cruel, though, and his execution of British prisoners gave me some splendid sequences. The second villain was, of course, Obadiah Hakeswill. I had stupidly killed him off in *Sharpe's Enemy*, but now, because I was going back to the beginning of Sharpe's career, I was able to resurrect Obadiah in all his glory.

Yet to look at Sergeant Hakeswill was to see the perfect soldier. It was true that his oddly lumpy face twitched every few seconds as though an evil spirit was twisting and jerking just beneath his sun-reddened skin, but his eyes were blue, his hair was powdered as white as the snow that never fell on this land, and his uniform was as smart as though he stood guard at Windsor Castle. He performed drill like a Prussian, each movement so crisp and clean that it was a pleasure to watch, but then the face would twitch and his oddly child-like eyes would flicker a sideways glance and you could see the devil peering out.

That passage was written with Pete Postlethwaite in mind. Peter Postlethwaite, of course, was the actor who played Hakeswill so brilliantly, and I could no longer use my earlier description of Hakeswill (from *Sharpe's Company*) because the actor had entirely redefined the character. I don't think Pete has blue eyes, but otherwise the 'new' Hakeswill is him. It was always a pleasure to write Obadiah, but in *Sharpe's Tiger* he fairly leaps at the reader.

"The men can talk, Sergeant,"

Lieutenant Lawford observed mildly. "The other companies aren't silent."

"No, sir! Must save their breath, sir! Too bleeding hot to talk, sir, and besides, sir, they've got heathens to kill, sir, mustn't waste breath on chit-chat, sir, not when there are black-faced heathens to kill, sir. Says so in the scriptures."

And that was Hakeswill's new line, 'says so in the scriptures', a mantra he repeats at every inappropriate moment. I wish, of course, that I had thought of it ten years earlier when I first wrote him, but at least it would serve Hakeswill through the Indian tales.

One of the joys of writing historical novels is to 'explain' the small dark inexplicable corners of real history. One of those mysteries is what caused the terrible explosion at Almeida, described in *Sharpe's Gold*, and another is how the Tippoo died. We know he was shot in the Watergate, a tunnel leading through Seringapatam's ramparts, but the British soldier who killed him was never discovered. He would have been rewarded, but he never volunteered his action, probably because the Tippoo, when he died, was festooned with jewels. That unknown soldier became very rich that day and he undoubtedly feared that his ill-gotten loot would be confiscated. So Sharpe takes his place.

The bullet went higher than Sharpe intended. He had thought to put it through the Tippoo's heart, but instead it struck the king in the temple. The Tippoo's head had been whipped back by the bullet's force and blood was soaking into his cloth-padded helmet, but he forced his head forward and stared into Sharpe's eyes, he seemed to smile before he slumped down.

The echo of the musket shot still battered Sharpe's ears so he was not aware that he was talking as he crouched beside the Tippoo. "It's your ruby I want," Sharpe said, "that bloody great ruby." The Tippoo still lived, but he could not move. His expressionless eyes stared up at Sharpe who thought the Tippoo was dead, but then the dying man blinked. "Still here, are you?" Sharpe asked. He patted the Tippoo's bloodied cheek. "You're a brave fat bastard, I'll say that for you." He wrenched the huge ruby off the blood-spattered feather plume, then stripped the dying man of every jewel he could find. He took the pearls from the Tippoo's neck, twisted off an armlet bright with gems, tugged off the diamond rings and unlatched the silver-hung necklace of emeralds. He pulled out the sash to see if the dagger with the great diamond called the Moonstone was there, but the sash held nothing.

He could not find the Moonstone, of course, or else Wilkie Collins could not have written the novel with that title. Sharpe becomes rich in the Watergate, but he has an annoying habit of losing his money, especially to women. So he kills the Tippoo, then he tries to kill Obadiah Hakeswill by feeding him to the Tippoo's tigers. Obadiah, of course, does not die ("I cannot die, says so in the scriptures,"). The various futile attempts Sharpe makes to murder Obadiah are a mild jest on the fact that Obadiah believes himself immortal, but they worried a lot of readers and I received numerous letters plaintively enquiring how Obadiah survived, in turn, hungry tigers, an enraged bull elephant and a pit of lethal snakes, and the sad truth is that I don't know. But Obadiah had to survive to crop up again in *Sharpe's Company*.

Sharpe begins *Sharpe's Tiger* as a private and ends it as a sergeant. He has also learned to read in the Tippoo's dungeons, so now he has two of the necessary qualifications to be promoted from the ranks.

That promotion occurs in the second Indian adventure, *Sharpe's Triumph*, which tells the extraordinary story of the battle of Assaye. And at the heart of that battle is another of those small mysteries. We know that Sir Arthur Wellesley, while galloping across the field from one wing of his army to the other, was stranded in the enemy gun line. His horse, Diomed, had been piked in the chest, the general slid from the saddle and was surrounded by his Mahratta enemies. He survived, yet he was ever reluctant to describe exactly what happened. In a career that was remarkable for his frequent proximity to mortal danger and his avoidance of anything other than the most trifling wounds, that survival was the Duke of Wellington's closest brush with death. Yet what happened? He would not say, but I needed an event that would catapult Sharpe into the officer's mess, and that event had to be a display of extraordinary bravery, and Wellesley's miraculous survival gave me the perfect opportunity. In all Sharpe's career that is the crucial moment. It brings him to Wellesley's notice, it makes him an officer and it begins his reputation, and for all those reasons it is worth reliving, albeit in a slightly abbreviated form. Sharpe, reluctantly, has replaced Sir Arthur Wellesley's orderly and is following the General across the battlefield and through the enemy gun line. For some good reason, which I cannot now remember,

Sergeant Sharpe is armed with a Light Cavalry sabre, while many of the enemy carry tulwars, an Indian sabre.

Sharpe saw the white stallion falling and sliding, and he saw Wellesley thrown forward onto the horse's neck. He saw the half-dozen enemy closing in for the kill, and suddenly the chaos and the terror of the day all vanished. Sharpe knew what he had to do, and knew it as clearly as though his whole life had been spent waiting for just this moment.

He kicked the roan mare straight at the enemy. He could not reach the General, for Wellesley was still in the saddle of the wounded Diomed who was sliding on the ground and trailing the pikestaff from his bleeding chest, and the threat of the horse's weight had driven the enemy aside, three to the left and three to the right. One fired his musket at Wellesley, but the ball flew wide, and then, as Diomed slowed, the Mahrattas closed in and it was then that Sharpe struck them. He used the mare as a battering ram, taking her perilously close to where the General had fallen from the saddle, and he drove her into the three gunners on the right, scattering them, and at the same time he kicked his feet from the stirrups and swung himself off the horse so that he fell beside the dazed Wellesley. Sharpe stumbled as he fell, but he came up from the ground snarling with the sabre sweeping wide at the three men he had charged, but they had been driven back by the mare's impact, and so Sharpe whipped back to see a gunner standing right over the General with a bayonet raised, ready to strike, and he lunged at the man, screaming at him, and he felt the sabre's tip tear through the muscles of the gunner's belly. Sharpe thrust the blade, toppling the gunner back onto Diomed's blood-flecked flank.

The sabre stuck in the wound. The gunner was thrashing, his musket fallen, and one of his comrades was climbing over Diomed with a tulwar in his hand. Sharpe heaved on the sabre, jerking the dying man, but the blade would not free itself of the flesh's suction and so he stepped over Wellesley, who was still dizzied and fallen, and put his left boot on the gunner's groin and heaved again. The man with the tulwar struck down and Sharpe felt a blow on his left shoulder, but then his own sabre came free and he swung it clumsily at his new attacker.

The man stepped back to avoid the blade and tripped on one of Diomed's rear legs. He fell. Sharpe turned, his sabre sweeping blindly wide with drops of blood flicking from its tip as he sought to drive back any enemy coming from his right. There was none, but Sharpe knew that both he and the General were going to die here if he did not find some shelter fast.

The big painted eighteen pounder gun offered some small safety and so Sharpe stooped, took hold of Wellesley's collar, and unceremoniously dragged the General towards the cannon. The General was not unconscious, for he clung to his slim straight sword, but he was half stunned and helpless. Two men ran to cut Sharpe off from the gun's sanctuary and he let go of the General's stiff collar and attacked the pair. "Bastards," he screamed as he fought them. Bugger the advice about straight-arm and parrying, this was a time to kill in sheer rage and he went for the two men in a berserk fury. The sabre was a clumsy weapon, but it was sharp and heavy and he almost severed the first man's neck and the subsequent back swing opened the second man's arm to the bone, and Sharpe turned back to Wellesley, who was still not recovered from his fall, and he saw an Arab lancer spurring his horse straight at the fallen General. Sharpe bellowed an obscenity at the man, then slashed the heavy sabre across the horse's face and the beast swerved wildly aside. Sharpe took Wellesley's collar again and hauled the General into the space between the gun's gaudy barrel and one of its gigantic wheels. "Stay there!" Sharpe snapped, then turned to see that the Arab lancer, out of his saddle now, was leading a charge of gunners. Sharpe went to meet them. He swept the lance aside with his sabre's blade, then rammed the weapon's bar-hilt into the Arab's face. He felt the man's nose break, kicked him in the balls, hacked down with the sabre, then turned to his left and sliced the blade within an inch of a gunner's eyes.

Sharpe had four men in front of him now, four men with bared teeth and bright weapons. Their eyes flicked from Sharpe to Wellesley. The Mahrattas did not know that they had the British General trapped, but they must have realised that he must be a senior officer because his red coat was bright with braid and lace,, and so they came to capture him, but first they had to get past Sharpe . . . . .

Sharpe seized a pike thrusting at his belly, pulled it towards him and met the oncoming pikeman with the sabre's tip. Straight into his throat. Sharpe's shoulder was bleeding, but there was no pain. He was keening a mad noise as he fought and it seemed to him at that instant as though he could do nothing wrong. It was as if the enemy had been magically slowed to half speed and he had been quickened. He was taller than any of them, and he was stronger, and he was suddenly much faster, He was even enjoying the fight, had he known anything of what he felt, but he only sensed the madness of battle; the sublime madness that drives out fear, dulls pain and drives a man close to ecstasy. He was screaming at the enemy, begging them to come and be killed.

Two came and Sharpe stepped towards them and used both his hands to bring the heavy sabre down in a savage cut that bit through the hat and skull of the nearest enemy. Sharpe screamed a curse at the dying man for his sabre was trapped in his skull, but he wrenched it free and sliced it right, a grey jelly sliding off its edge, to drive the second man back . . . more were coming. Christ knows how many bastards there were, but Sharpe did not care. He had come to fight and God had given him one screaming hell of a battle.

There is more, of course, much more, before Wellesley is safe. In a more recent book, *Sharpe's Fury*, Sharpe is asked how many men he killed during that rescue and he cannot remember. He thinks it was five. I have just re-read the whole passage and reckon he was right, it was five, but he forgot two 'possibles' so it could have been seven. It was one of Sharpe's finest moments, and from it sprang his career and the rest of the series.

He becomes an officer at the end of *Sharpe's Triumph*, an Ensign in the 74th, a Scottish regiment that does not really want him. That tale of his unhappy introduction to commissioned rank is told in *Sharpe's Fortress*, the last of the Indian stories, and by the end of the book Sharpe has been offered a chance to join a new-fangled regiment forming in England, the 95th, and that will mean discarding his red coat and donning a green jacket. He does not want to discard the red coat, but decides he has little choice.

Sharpe stood and watched the 74th march in. They had not wanted him   because he was not a gentleman, but, by God, he was a soldier, and he had opened the fort for them. He caught Urquhart's eye, and Urquhart looked at the blood on Sharpe's face and at the crusting scabs on Sharpe's sword, then looked away. "Good afternoon, Urquhart," Sharpe said loudly.

Urquhart spurred his horse.

"Good afternoon, Sergeant Colquhoun," Sharpe said.

Colquhoun marched doggedly on.

Sharpe smiled. He had proved that he was a soldier, but he had always known that. He was a soldier and he would stay a soldier, and if that meant wearing the green jacket instead of the red, then so be it. But he was a soldier, and he had proved that in the heat and blood of Gawilghur. It was the fastness in the sky, the stronghold that could not fall, and now it was Sharpe's fortress.

*　　*　　*

Sharpe, of course, had to return from India, and it occurred to me, somewhat mischievously, that his homeward voyage must inevitably take him not far from Cape Trafalgar and, as his last fight in India was in 1804 and because the battle of Trafalgar was fought in 1805, it seemed an irresistible mischief. Hornblower, after all, never got to Trafalgar, but why should Sharpe not fight there? And the result, *Sharpe's Trafalgar*, is one of my favourite books. The main reason for that is Lady Grace, wife of Lord William Hale, whom Sharpe first glimpses ashore in Bombay.

> She was much younger than Lord William and her pale, slender face had a haunting beauty, almost a sadness, that struck Sharpe with the force of a bullet. He stared at her, entranced by her. He could not take his eyes from her ladyship, for she was truly beautiful; breathtakingly, achingly, untouchably beautiful. Her face was pale as ivory, sharp-shadowed . . .

Lady Grace appears snobbish, cold, haughty, distant and privileged. She is a piece of 'upper-class totty' and the phrase is not mine, but came from one of the three people who, at a convention of the Sharpe Appreciation Society separately told me it was high time Sharpe met and fell in love with a piece of upper-class totty. When three people give the same message it is time to listen, so I dreamed up Lady Grace and made her appear utterly unapproachable. Sharpe, of course, is doomed to fall in love the moment he sees her. He pursues her, suspecting that his pursuit is futile, but Lady Grace is not all she appears to be.

She laughed and her face, for the first time since Sharpe had met her, was filled with life and he thought he had never seen, nor ever would see, a woman so lovely. So lovely that Sharpe stepped forward and kissed her. She pushed him away and he stepped back, mortified, readying incoherent apologies, but she was only extricating her arms that had been trapped between their bodies and once they were free she snaked them about his neck and pulled his face to hers and kissed him so fiercely that Sharpe tasted blood from her lip. She sighed, then placed her cheek against his. "Oh, God," she said softly, "I wanted you to do that since the moment I first saw you."

She is one of my favourite heroines, and therein is a huge problem. I was now well embarked on a second Sharpe series that would have to dovetail with the first. Dovetail is too precise a word. It is bodging carpentry, to be honest. If Sharpe was at Trafalgar, why does he never mention it in later adventures? And the worst aspect is that if you invent a heroine like Lady Grace and if she and Sharpe fall head over heels in love, then why is she not in the later books? There is really only one answer, which is that she has to die. That is horrible, but inevitable, and a consequence of writing the books out of order.

I received a half dozen letters after
Sharpe's Trafalgar, all of them complaining
to me that Sharpe would never have killed
Malachi Braithwaite. To set the scene, Malachi
Braithwaite, 'an Oxford man', is Lord William
Hale's confidential secretary and, during the
voyage from India to Trafalgar, he discovers
that his master's wife is being unfaithful with
Sharpe. He tries to blackmail her. Sharpe
discovers the blackmail and solves it neatly
enough by murdering Braithwaite. And, being
Sharpe, he cannot keep it simple, but tries to
discover how hard it is to wring a man's neck
like a chicken. A fairly futile exercise, you
might think, but Sharpe had seen the Tippoo's
jettis kill men in that manner and he wanted
to know if it was difficult.

Sharpe was holding the
secretary's arms above his back,
pushing them painfully forward, and
now he shoved them hard to dislocate
both shoulders. Braithwaite gave a
whimper of pain, then screamed as
Sharpe gripped one of his ears and
turned his head sideways. Sharpe
was trying to find a purchase with
his right hand on Braithwaite's face
and Braithwaite tried to bite him, so
Sharpe smacked his face then gripped
a handful of head and ear and twisted
the head hard. "God knows how they

did it," Sharpe said, "those bloody jettis, but I watched them so it must be possible."

It is possible, and it is also murder, plain and simple, and that crime upset a surprising number of readers. Now it is very flattering when readers feel they know a character well enough to protest about behaviour they find unworthy of him, but to tell me that Sharpe is not a murderer? Of course he is. He's a murderer, a thief and a rogue, but the point of him is that he's our rogue. He is on our side. Sharpe would indeed murder someone, especially for a woman's sake, and I have to say that none of the letter-writers was a woman. Women know a good man when they see one, and Lady Grace finds happiness with Sharpe. A retired soldier, who had been a Warrant Officer in the Scots Guards, and who, when I met him, was running a programme for teenaged drug addicts, told me that 'a soldier fights battles for those who cannot fight for themselves.' I think that is the most brilliant summation of a soldier's purpose that I have ever heard, and I have used it in the Sharpe books more than once. Sharpe fights for those who cannot fight for themselves, and he also fights dirty. That's why I like him. So my correspondents were wrong; Sharpe would murder for a woman's sake, and he did, and most probably will again.

Two years after Trafalgar the British were fighting very dirtily in, of all places, Denmark, and that campaign formed the background to *Sharpe's Prey*. I confess here that, as time goes on, it becomes more and more difficult to find titles for the Sharpe books, and *Sharpe's Prey* is really fairly meaningless, except that it's a tribute to John Sandford's series of Prey books which I admire enormously. I am not even sure who the prey of the title is, but whatever, the story is set in Denmark where, in 1807, a small British army and a large British fleet go to force the Danes into surrendering their own fleet. This was naked aggression and very hard-edged politics. The Danes had a huge fleet to protect their large merchant marine, and now that Napoleon had lost virtually all his battleships at Trafalgar it was feared that the French would invade Denmark and simply take the Danish fleet as replacements for the ships they had lost to Nelson. The Danes were asked to send all their warships to Britain where they would be kept safe for the war's duration. The Danes, quite properly, refused, so the British forced them. It was an ugly little war, made uglier by the ruthless bombardment of Copenhagen.

The city surrendered next morning. Seven thousand bombs had fallen in the night and some of the streets blazed so fiercely that no one could get within a hundred paces. Charred pages of the university's library had rained across a hundred square miles of Zealand, while the cathedral was a gaunt frame of scorched stone in which heaps of embers smoked like the pit. Bodies lay in neat rows in parks, squares and on the harbour quays. There were not nearly enough coffins, so folk whose homes were undamaged brought their sheets and did their best to make the dead decent.

Some 1,600 citizens of Copenhagen were killed by the bombardment, a precursor of the horrors to come in the twentieth century. It is a strangely forgotten episode (at least by the British). Many people know of Nelson's attack on Copenhagen in 1801, but the later, and far more damaging assault has faded from memory, or at least from British memory. I could only find one account of the bombardment written by an inhabitant of the city and that account was in Danish, which I do not speak, but fortuitously, during the summer that I was writing *Sharpe's Prey*, some Danish friends came to visit us in Cape Cod. I sat them down with the memoir and asked them to translate it aloud for me. This they dutifully did until the missiles began to fall on the first night of the bombardment, after which the account was punctuated with exclamations. "You British are so terrible! This is awful! How could you do it to us?" Well, we did, and we denied Napoleon the possibility of capturing the Danish fleet for himself, but it was still a monstrous act of bullying. There's a curious footnote to the campaign. Sir Arthur Wellesley was the General commanding the British army on the expedition and, while he was in Denmark, the mare of another British general was found to be pregnant. She was sent back to Britain where she foaled a stallion which eventually came into Wellesley's possession. The horse, which he rode throughout the battle of Waterloo, was called Copenhagen.

Then, suddenly, there was no place to take Sharpe except back to Portugal and Spain, so from now on the books are interpolated between the early Sharpe adventures. On the whole this means that the stories must use lesser known events in the Peninsular War. The first series scooped up most of the big battles like Talavera, Badajoz, Salamanca and Vitoria, but it is surprising how much was left over, more than enough, certainly, for what is shaping up to be a second Sharpe series. *Sharpe's Havoc* was the first book to take Sharpe back to Portugal and it tells of the fighting in Oporto and in the country to the north. The book begins with the French occupation of Oporto and the horror that followed the breaking of a pontoon bridge across the River Douro. The bridge was crammed with refugees fleeing the French and, when it broke, hundreds were drowned.

The central hundred feet of the bridge were now under water. Those hundred feet had been swept clear of people, but more were being forced into the gap that suddenly churned white as the drawbridge was sheared away from the rest of the bridge by the river's pressure. The great span of the bridge turned, reared up black, turned over and was swept seawards, and now there was no bridge across the Douro, but the people on the northern bank still did not know the roadway was cut and so they kept pushing and bullying their way onto the sagging bridge and those in front could not hold them back and instead were inexorably pushed into the broken gap where the white water seethed on the bridge's shattered ends. The cries of the crowd grew louder, and the sound only increased the panic so that more and more people struggled towards the place where the refugees drowned. Gun smoke, driven by an errant gust of wind, dipped into the gorge and whirled above the bridge's broken centre where desperate people thrashed at the water as they were swept downstream. Gulls screamed and wheeled. Some Portuguese troops were now trying to hold the French in the streets of the city, but it was a hopeless endeavour. They were outnumbered, the enemy had the high ground, and more and more French forces were flooding down the hill. The screams of the fugitives on the bridge was like the sound of the doomed on the Day of Judgement, the cannon balls were booming overhead, the streets of the city were echoing with musket shots, hooves were echoing from house walls and flames were crackling in buildings broken apart by cannon fire.

"Those wee children." Harper said, "God help them." The orphans, in their dun uniforms were being pushed into the river. "There's got to be a bloody boat!"

But the men manning the barges had rowed themselves to the south bank and abandoned their craft and so there were no boats to rescue the drowning, just horror in a cold grey river and a line of small heads being swept downstream in the fretting waves and there was nothing

Sharpe could do. He could not reach the bridge and though he shouted at folk to abandon the crossing they did not understand English. Musket balls were flecking the river now and some were striking the fugitives on the broken bridge.

"What the hell can we do?" Harper asked.

"Nothing," Sharpe said harshly, "except get out of here."

I find it very touching that if you visit Oporto today you can find, on the river quay, a small shrine to that tragedy. It seems to be replenished daily with flowers and candles even though the disaster occurred in 1809.

The recapture of Oporto by Sir Arthur Wellesley (yet to be renamed Wellington) is a magnificent tale. The French, for a long time, were convinced that he was an effective defensive general, but lacked the panache and audacity to be a great attacking commander. This was always a ridiculous opinion (though strangely it persists). Oporto proved them wrong for he took an enormous risk in throwing a handful of men across the river after the fortuitous discovery of some barges. Those few men garrisoned a seminary which still stands, and thereby threatened Marshal Soult's rear. Sharpe, of course, is responsible for discovering those barges, but because he has been a fugitive for some days, is utterly ignorant of what else is happening in Portugal.

"So what's happening, sir?" Sharpe asked.

"Happening?" Colonel Waters said, "we're running the Frogs out of Portugal! Hop, hop, croak, croak, and good bloody riddance to the spavined bastards. Look at it!" Waters gestured through the window to the French held city. "They don't have the first blind idea that we're here! Your Portuguese fellow said you'd been cut off. Is that true?"

"Since the end of March," Sharpe said.

"Ye Gods," Waters said, "you must be out of touch!" The Colonel perched on the window sill from where he told Sharpe that Sir Arthur Wellesley had arrived in Portugal. "He came less than three weeks ago," Waters said, "and he's put some snap into the troops, by God, he has! Cradock was a decent enough fellow, but he had no snap, none! So we're on the march, Sharpe, left, right, left, right, and the devil take the hindmost."

The French were tumbled out of Oporto and then harried north out of Portugal altogether, and Marshal Soult's whole army might have been captured had a blocking force moved with greater speed towards the one road left on which the French could retreat. As it was the French lost all their guns and baggage. It was a remarkable operation, and one that should have taught the French to be more cautious when facing Sir Arthur Wellesley.

Yet Napoleon wanted Portugal, and it must have seemed an easy enough morsel to be swallowed after his armies had cowed and taken much of the rest of Europe. Britain's army in Portugal was very small, the French forces were large, and after Soult's defeat the next invasion was led by Marshal Massena. He attacked in the south of Portugal just one year after Soult's defeat in the north. That campaign forms the basis of *Sharpe's Escape* which, unusually for a Sharpe book, begins with the big set-piece battle rather than ending with it. That battle was Busaco, where Wellesley dared the French to assault his position at the top of a long, steep ridge, and the French took the dare. It was an extraordinary risk by Massena, and an unnecessary one because a road looped about the north of the Busaco ridge and, when he eventually took that road, he forced Wellesley to continue his retreat. But before that Massena tried to sweep the British and Portuguese from his path by attacking the ridge with thirty-three battalions. They attacked, as ever, in columns.

Officers gave orders, sergeants bellowed, shoved, and used their musket stocks to force men into the ranks, and some fools mistook their orders and joined the wrong column, and they had to be pulled out, cursed, and sent to their proper place, but eventually the thirty three battalions were assembled in their four assault columns in the small meadows beside the stream.

There were eighteen thousand men in the four columns. If those men had been paraded in a line of three ranks, which was how the French made their lines, they would have stretched for two miles, but instead they had been concentrated into the four tight columns. The two largest led the attack, while the two smaller came behind, ready to exploit whatever opening the first two made. Those two larger columns had only forty men in their front ranks, but there were forty more ranks behind and the great blocks made two battering rams, almost two miles of infantry concentrated into two moving squares that were designed to be hammered against the enemy line and overwhelm it by sheer weight. "Stay close!" The sergeants shouted as they began to ascend the ridge. A column was no good if it lost cohesion. To work it had to be like a machine, every man in step, shoulder to shoulder, the rear ranks pushing the front rank on into the enemy guns. That front rank would probably die, as would the one behind, and the one behind that, but eventually the impetus of the massive formation should force it across their own dead and through the enemy line and then the real killing could begin. The battalions' drummers were concentrated at the centre of each column and the boys played the fine rhythm of the charge, pausing every so often to let the men call out the refrain, *"Vive l'Empereur!"*

That refrain became breathless as the columns climbed. The ridge was horribly steep, lung-sapping, and men tired and so began to lag and stray. The fog was still thick. Scattered gorse bushes and stunted trees obstructed the columns that split to pass them, and after a while the fragments did not join up again, but just struggled up through the silent fog, wondering what waited for them at the summit. Before they were half way up the hill both the leading columns had each broken into groups of tired men, and the officers, swords drawn, were shouting at the groups to form ranks, to hurry, and the officers shouted from different parts of the hill and only confused the troops more so that they went first one way and then the other. The drummer boys, following the broken ranks, beat more slowly as they grew more tired.

A column is simply a block of men, usually much wider than it is deep, so calling it a column, though correct, is slightly misleading. The word 'column' suggests a formation shaped like a battering ram, but it is more like a bulldozer's blade. A French battalion had six companies (as against the British ten) and if they attacked in column of divisions they would have three companies in front and three behind. They were in close order, shoulder to shoulder, and a bird's eye view would show nine ranks of around seventy men each (a rough estimate, depending, of course, on just how many men were in the battalion.) So the column is seventy men wide and nine deep, and the obvious drawback of that formation is that almost all of the men in the rearward eight ranks are unable to use their muskets. Only the front rank can fire safely, and perhaps the men in the outside files. So our notional battalion, attacking a British battalion of equal size, can bring around eighty muskets to bear. If the second rank can fire safely while marching then you can double that figure, but it still means that only about one hundred and fifty muskets are threatening the British, who will be waiting for them in a line of two ranks. So every British musket can fire, and seven hundred muskets are always going to defeat one hundred and fifty.

So why did the French persist in using columns? There were two reasons. The first was that the column had been successful all across Europe. It had a real psychological advantage. The sight of a great mass of men inexorably advancing tended to demoralise opposing troops, and time and again the columns had taken their punishment, kept going, and the enemy panicked and fled from their threat. The second reason was that much of the French army was composed of conscripts; young men plucked unwillingly from their civilian jobs, dressed in blue, given a musket, and marched to war. It was easy to train such men to advance in a column, much easier than teaching them to fight in a more extended order. The problem the French faced, right up to and including Waterloo, was that the British army excelled in musketry and was not overawed by the column, so the British routinely out-shot the French column.

The Emperor himself recognised this danger and grumbled that his marshals insisted on deploying columns against British lines without first weakening the line with artillery fire, but that, I think, was arguing after the event. Wellington was a master at protecting his infantry from artillery and, even at Waterloo, after a massive artillery bombardment, the British line saw off the Emperor's columns. The other weapon to deploy against the line was *voltigeurs*, 'vaulters', the French light troops who skirmished ahead of the column. They were in loose order and their job was to fire at the line, but of course they were opposed by British light troops whose job was to dispose of the *voltigeurs*. They came on the same old way, Wellington said of the Emperor's troops at Waterloo, and we saw them off in the same old way. That 'old way' was demonstrated at Busaco.

"Present!" Lawford shouted, and nearly six hundred muskets went into mens' shoulders.

"Fire!"

The massive volley pumped out a long cloud of gunsmoke that smelt like rotting eggs, and then the musket stocks thumped onto the ground and men took new cartridges and began to reload. "Platoon fire now!" Lawford called to his officers, and he took off his hat again and wiped sweat from his forehead. It was still cold, the wind blowing chill from the far off Atlantic, yet Lawford was hot. Sharpe heard the splintering crack of the Portuguese volley, then the South Essex began their own rolling fire, shooting half company by half company from the centre of the line, the bullets never ending, the men going through the well practised motions of loading and firing, loading and firing. The enemy was invisible now, hidden from the battalion by its own gun smoke. Sharpe rode along the right of the line, deliberately not going left so no one could accuse him of interfering with Slingsby. "Aim low!" he called to the men, "aim low!" A few bullets were coming back out of the smoke, but they were nearly all high. Inexperienced men usually shot high and the French, who were being flayed by the Portuguese and by the South Essex, were trying to fire uphill into a cloud of smoke and they were taking a terrible punishment from muskets and cannons. Some of the enemy must be panicking because Sharpe saw two ramrods go wheeling overhead, evidence that the men were too scared to remember their musket drill. He stopped by the grenadier company and watched the Portuguese and he reckoned they were firing as efficiently as any redcoat battalion. Their half company volleys were steady as clockwork, the smoke rolling out from the battalion's centre and he knew the bullets must be striking hard into the disintegrating column's face.

More muskets flared as the 88th, the feared Connaught Rangers, wheeled forward of the line to blast at the wounded French column, but somehow the French held on. Their outer ranks and files were being killed and wounded, but the mass of men inside the column still lived and more were climbing the hill to replace the dead, and the whole mass, in no good order, but crowding together, still tried to advance into the terrible volleys. More red and brown jacketed troops were moving towards the fight, adding their musketry, but still the French pushed against the storm. The column was dividing again, torn by the slashing round shots and ripped by canister so now it seemed as though disorganised groups of men were struggling uphill past piles of dead. Sharpe could hear the officers and sergeants shouting them on, could hear the rattle of the frantic drums that was now challenged by a British band that was playing Men of Harlech.

The columns are defeated, Massena has failed, but still Wellesley had to retreat because he is so fearfully outnumbered, but *Sharpe's Escape* tells of the great surprise of the Lines of Torres Vedras which Wellesley had built to prevent the French reaching Lisbon. The lines (a succession of massive forts and scarped hillsides stretching across the wide peninsula north of Lisbon) worked and Napoleon's ambition to be master of the whole Atlantic coastline was frustrated.

Sharpe's Escape was the twentieth novel in the series. I am frequently asked how many more there will be and I always answer five. I said that when there were only five novels in print, again when there were six, and so on. I say five because it is an easier answer than trying to work out the real answer which is that I do not know. I only know there will be more stories, and some, like the twenty-first, will surprise me. Judy and I were invited to a wedding in Jerez de la Frontera, a town not far from Cadiz in southern Spain, and a long way from any place where Wellington fought. But close to Cadiz is Barrosa, a small seaside resort, and it was at Barrosa that the British, under the leadership of Sir Thomas Graham, captured the first of the many French eagles they were to take in the wars. I thought it would be interesting to see the battlefield, even though it had nothing whatever to do with Sharpe or Wellington, and so, under the influence of a massive hangover (Spanish weddings are spectacular), we drove to Barrosa. There is almost nothing left of the battlefield now, but I stood on the hill where Major Browne's makeshift battalion marched to certain death and I looked past the construction cranes on the lower ground where Major Gough's Irish took the eagle of the French 8th, and I thought Sharpe has to be here. I had no idea how to get him to Cadiz, but the thought of writing Barrosa was irresistible, and so *Sharpe's Fury* was born. Sharpe never got onto the hill with Browne, as I initially thought he would, but instead fights near Gough's Irishmen, but a tale of the hill will show how terrible that battle beside the sea was.

Major Browne walked up and down behind his line. It was not much of a line. Ranks and files were gone, blown to ragged ruin by the artillery or blasted by the musket balls, but the living had not retreated. They were shooting back. Loading and firing, making small clouds of smoke that hid them from the enemy. Their mouths were sour from the saltpetre of the gunpowder and their cheeks burned by sparks from the locks. Wounded men struggled up to join the line where they loaded and fired. "Well done, my boys!" Browne shouted, "well done!" He expected to die. He was sad about that, but his duty was to stay on his feet, to walk the line, to shout encouragement and to wait for the canister or musket ball that must end his life. "Come cheer up, my lads!' he sang, "'tis to glory we steer, to add something more to this wonderful year; to honour we call you, not press you like slaves, for who are so free as the sons of the waves?" A corporal fell back, brains spilling from his forehead. The man must have been dead, but his mouth still moved compulsively until Browne leaned down and pushed the chin gently up. He walked on. "You're holding them, boys!" he shouted, "you're holding them!"

And that was true. The French had broken Browne's attack. They had shattered the red ranks, they had ripped the Gibraltar Flankers apart, but the French were not advancing down the slope to where Browne's survivors would have made easy meat for their bayonets. They fired instead, tearing more bullets into the broken battalion while the redcoats, the men from Lancashire and the Holy Boys from Norfolk and the Silver-Tails from Gloucestershire, shot back. Major Browne watched them die. A boy from the Silver-Tails reeled back with his left shoulder torn away by the razor-edged remnants of the canister's casing so that his arm hung by sinews and broken ribs poked white through the red mess of his shattered chest. He collapsed and began to gasp for his mother. Browne knelt and held the boy's hand. He wanted to stanch the wound, but it was too big, and so the Major, not knowing how else to comfort the dying soldier, sang to him.

Barrosa, like all the other books, is a tribute to the heroism of the British soldier. There is an odd idea (I heard it being trotted out by a professor on Radio Four not long ago) that Wellington's army was a mass of gutter-born scum commanded by aristocrats and disciplined by brutality. That is glib rubbish. You cannot win wars with such an instrument. There were very few aristocrats, most of the officers were what we would call middle-class, and by the war's end many, like Sharpe, had been promoted from the ranks. The army's morale was high and memoir after memoir shows that there was mutual respect between officers and men. They joked, they survived, they did endure terrible punishments from time to time, but they fought like devils and they won battle after battle. Sharpe is one of them.

I have lived with Sharpe now for almost thirty years, longer if I count the days when he was just an unnamed dream. I often wonder what would have happened if Judy had not emerged from that lift in an Edinburgh hotel. I assume I would have stayed in television and Sharpe would have remained a dream, but Judy did appear and with her came a grumpy Rifleman scowling at the world. I do like Sharpe, but am not at all sure he would like me. In *Sharpe's Fury* there is a writer, Benito Chavez (the coincidence of the initials is deliberate) and Chavez is, I think, the closest I have tried for a self portrait: 'a miserable creature, a whining, smoke-ridden, alcohol-sodden, sweat-stinking excuse for a man, a writer.' But the two of us have spent almost thirty happy years together, and there is always a joy when I confront an empty page and know that Sharpe is about to appear. For me it is like meeting an old friend, and he and I have many stories yet to share for his adventures are not over. I do not know how many more battles he will have to fight, five perhaps? But one thing is certain. Sharpe and Harper will march again.

Cakes and Ale

A Cautionary Note!!!

I am sometimes asked, I have no idea why, about my religious beliefs. I have none. Recently a reader wrote wanting reassurance that Sharpe was a Christian! He is not. Religion enters fairly prominently in my books, for the simple reason that any pre-technological society is more religious than a world in which God's mysterious ways have been explained by science. Yet my interest in religion is more personal than that. I was brought up in a very religious household, and the influence of that upbringing has cast a long shadow into the novels. This essay is an account of that childhood and those who revere the Christian religion might well find parts of it offensive. You have been warned.

My birth mother, Dorothy Cornwell, nursed me for two weeks. It was 1944, she was twenty years old, unmarried and her father insisted she had to give me up, but she nevertheless kept me for that fortnight in the institution where she had been sent to have her baby. When I was ten days old a couple arrived and stood at the foot of the bed from where they inspected the two of us. "I could tell they weren't cuddly," Dorothy has since told me. She was right.

"Do you know who the boy's father is?" Uncuddly Marjorie asked.

"His name is Oughtred."

"Oughtred!" Pause. "He's not French, is he? Because if he's French we don't want the boy."

Alas, William Oughtred was Canadian and, four days later, I was taken from Hackney to Benfleet in Essex. My name, which had been recorded as Bernard Cornwell on my birth certificate, was changed to Bernard Wiggins.

The Wiggins belonged to a sect called the Peculiar People. It was founded in the mid-nineteenth century, flourished in Essex for a hundred years and is now, happily, defunct. The name derived from the Bible where, in both the old and the new testaments, God describes his adherents as 'a peculiar people', meaning, simply, separate from all others, and the Peculiars of Essex believed that by keeping themselves separate from a sinful world they might avoid temptation and so attain salvation. Joseph Wiggins, my adoptive father, took me, I think, as a Christian duty. He considered me, and the four other children he adopted, as souls to be saved. Marjorie just wanted babies. She liked babies.

The Peculiars were fundamentalists, by which I mean that they took every word in the Authorised Version of Bible to be true. 'The prayer of faith shall save the sick,' says the Epistle of James, and so the early Peculiars refused medical attention, relying instead on anointing with oil and the laying on of hands. This, for a time, sufficed, but in 1908 the Children's Act declared that to refuse medical attention to a child was tantamount to criminal neglect, and so some Peculiars, preferring their children to die in the Lord rather than be attended by a doctor, were committed to prison. Others caved in, and the sect split into the Old and the New Peculiars. By the time I joined the faithful the split had healed, and my family, like most, had adopted a compromise solution by which the church elders were summoned to a sick person's bedside and, if God failed to perform the requisite miracle, then a doctor was called. One of my earliest memories is of a group of men clustered about my bed, their hands pressing rhythmically onto my forehead, earnestly beseeching Almighty God to heal me. God did not come through and so Dr Acres did the business instead.

Medicine was not the only thing of which the Peculiars disapproved. Alcohol, tobacco, cosmetics, the cinema, military service, comics, high heels, Roman Catholics, dancing, playing cards, gambling, television, the list was endless and was endlessly adaptable for anything considered frivolous was also reckoned sinful, and the immediate object of our lives was to avoid sin. There was a mysterious 'sin against the Holy Ghost' that loomed large in my young life for this sin, I never did discover what it was, was unforgivable and doomed the sinner to hell. Repentance would not help. There was no salvation. For a time I believed masturbation must be this sin, but I could not ask, for sex was, of course, the sinister unacknowledged beast that lurked behind the Peculiars' many fears. I also believed, for a time, that I had single-handedly, or double-handedly perhaps, discovered masturbation, and was quite happy to risk hell to enjoy it, but sticky sheets were my undoing and the inevitable punishment followed.

Stick and carrot. The carrot was the prospect of heaven and, more immediately, the bliss that would follow conversion. Conversion was important to the Peculiars. You gave your heart to Jesus, were washed in the blood of the lamb, went to the mercy seat, accepted Christ as your saviour and, miracle of miracles, became Happy! "I'm H - A - P - P -Y," we chirruped in Sunday School, "I'm H - A - P - P -Y! I know I am, I'm sure I am, I'm H - A - P - P -Y!" Except I was not and yearned to be, and for a long time I believed my route to happiness lay in conversion. I tried. I tried so hard. I became a serial heart donor for Jesus, but the happiness never arrived. Life did not suddenly become easier, I was not filled with a gleeful certainty, I felt no different, the emotion engendered by the threats of hell fire evaporated overnight and I was still the same sinful beast. The carrot of heaven failed to entice me onto the narrow path of righteousness and so the stick was produced to beat me up it.

The stick was always a bamboo garden stake, about a yard long, plucked from the fruit cage and wielded by my father, Joseph. He was a tall man, strongly built. At school, where I was caned often enough, the usual punishment was six swishes on the arse which stung a bit, but I was immune to such feeble assaults for I had experienced the Wrath of God administered by the garden stake. There was a ritual to these punishments, which began with me being locked into my bedroom and given time to reflect on my sins. Then would come the footsteps on the stairs. My father would unlock the door and order me to strip naked, after which he beat me in a frenzy compounded of dislike, righteous fury and despair for my soul. Afterwards, all passion spent, he would ask me to kneel and pray with him. I was thirteen or fourteen the last time it happened and Dr Acres had to be called. By the time he arrived the blood had been washed from the bedroom walls and the bedding had been changed, but there was no disguising the stigmata. I think the doctor offered my parents a warning because thereafter the bamboo stayed in its cage.

Was there no happiness? Of course there was. I remember playing Monopoly and I had an elaborate electric train layout and Arthur Mee's Children's Encyclopaedia, and there were Dinky toys and I had a big Meccano set which I liked and which pleased my father because he wanted me to take over the family's building firm when I grew up. Saint Paul had been a tentmaker, he told me often, and this was biblical authority for the truism that every Christian should have a useful trade. A practical trade. My father had left school at eleven, become a bricklayer and prospered until he employed over two hundred men. He preached to them in their lunch breaks and had the happy vision that I would follow in his footsteps. I see that in this paragraph my footsteps have wandered from the opening question; was there no happiness?

Yes, there was, but it was forever threatened by the fear of God and by Joe and Marjorie's marriage which was not happy.

The house was unhappy. Joseph was haunted by God while Marjorie was a bitter woman. I learned to fear the all too frequent sound of my parents' voices raised in argument for I had discovered that punishment inevitably followed such rows. I would lie in bed, hear the shouting downstairs and dread the dawn. The family prayers, in which, each morning, we read the bible aloud around the table and then bowed our heads as Joseph prayed, would be sullen. Storm cones hoisted.

They adopted five children. The eldest, John, was a dozen years older than I and I knew very little of him. He vanished one day. Despairing of making him into a Christian my parents had somehow contrived, I think without the help of the courts, into placing him in a Salvation Army reform home in South Wales. He would kill himself eventually. The youngest, Andrew, was much younger than I and by the time he was adopted I had left home. That left three of us, me sandwiched between two girls, Margaret and Ruth. Margaret, a couple of years older than me, was the favourite. She embraced the teaching of the Peculiar People and, though she was later to find refuge in the theologically suspect pastures of the Baptist church, remains a Christian. She is saved. Good for her, but she was no ally of mine. Ruth, a couple of years younger, was an ally, but we were easily divided and conquered. Survival was an individual thing, and my route was through hiding and lying. The first could delay punishment and the second could obviate it altogether and so I became a superb liar, able to separate a score or more of the tangled web's strands, and this facility, I think, has been of great use to me as a fiction writer. And when I was not telling lies I was fantasising, another useful accomplishment for a novelist.

I knew I was adopted from the very start. At about seven years old I was told by Marjorie that she wished she had not adopted me, a position from which she did not budge, and this was a consolation. I knew I did not belong. To what I belonged I did not know, but I knew it was not the Peculiars, and I was thus freed to construct my own parentage. This freedom was constrained at the age of eleven when my father left his safe open for a few moments and I dived in, hoping no doubt to find some of those big, beautiful five pound notes, and instead discovered a piece of paper on which my mother had written my natural parents' names and whatever other details she had learned of them. Dorothy Cornwell of East London and William Oughtred, Royal

Canadian Air Force, of British Columbia. A cockney and an airman. In truth I rejected Dorothy and William from the fantasies because they did not fit. I suppose I conjured up a duke and a showgirl? A princess? I cannot remember now. Today, of course, information like that written on the paper I discovered in Joseph's safe would be hidden behind a bureaucratic fence, but things had been different in wartime. Marjorie, when she married, was the assistant matron of an orphanage and had a professional relationship with the home where Dorothy gave birth, and so Marjorie was able to discover whence her babies came.

I hid the information. Years later I found the paper again and I briefly considered looking for Dorothy and William, but did nothing. I liked having no parents by then. Later still, as I approached my 60th birthday, I did find them, but by then I had no need of parents and it was safe to approach them. I met William first. I was fifty eight, he was eighty, and he was the patriarch of a large, happy family. I met them all, father, two half brothers, half sister, nieces and nephews, in Victoria, British Columbia, and had the extraordinary shock of recognition. I was like them. I looked like them, snorted like them when I laughed, and was immediately comfortable with them. I remember standing on William's terrace above the San Juan Straits and looking into his living room. It was late dusk, the lights were on and I could see them and they could not see me, and I just stared as they talked and laughed with my wife. This was family and I sensed Marjorie squirming in her grave because I had escaped. The same thing happened when, later, I met Dorothy and one of my four half brothers in England. My tribe. Like me.

Joseph was a good man, a very good man. He wanted heaven for us. He was honest, hard-working, earnest and wrong. He took me to Rayleigh once, a town not far from where we lived, and in the High Street there was, perhaps still is, a small monument to some Protestant martyrs burned there by Queen Mary. "One day, son," he told me solemnly, "I shall be burned here." I was seven or eight years old and did not know what to say. "The Pope and the communists will kill me," he claimed, and went on to explain that this unholy alliance was foretold in the bible which prophesied that the legions of Rome would unite with the red horde to extirpate the true faith from England. He believed that, just as he believed that God had cunningly placed the fossils in the geological record to test our faith. He was an unhappy man. At ten years old I stood outside his study, it was late dusk, the lights were on, and I could see him and he could not see me, and I watched him pray. He was in agony. He contorted himself. He raised his arms to God, beat them on his breast, he wept, he was pleading. Years after I recognised him in John Donne's lines, 'Batter my heart, three person'd God . . . o'erthrow me, and bend Your force to break, blow, burn and make me new.' He was in agony, yet he had done everything right. He had succeeded in business, given his soul to Jesus, rescued five other souls from sin, and he was unhappy, so angrily unhappy, and yet beneath the grim carapace of duty was a generous man capable of joy. But he had been born to and raised in the Peculiars and their puritanism was an inescapable part of his nature.

My nature derives from Dorothy and William. Theirs was an unlikely romance, ill-founded on lust and unrealistic hopes, but both are easy-going, humorous and tolerant. Life, they believe, is well lubricated by laughter. Neither, I think, want to delve too deeply into motives or philosophy and both, I know, are unbelievers. Perhaps I merely ascribe to them my own nature, but I am certain we cannot escape nature and that nurture is, at best, a minor influence. The Wiggins family, in its unscientific way, was a small experiment in nature versus nurture. Five of us were plucked from adulterous parents and put in a home where a rigid code of behaviour was fiercely enforced, and the result? God, one: the devil, four. Joseph, Marjorie and their eldest son are all dead now, and those of us who remain are not family. We do not see each other, do not write, have no ties.

The adoption failed. A family failed to ignite. All of us were unhappy. I live now in the USA where I am friends of a couple who have adopted two children. One of those children, a daughter, was born to a love affair which failed. Her birth mother reluctantly gave her up for adoption and then, a year or so later, was reunited with her lover. The two married, had more children, thrived, and, of course, felt remorseful about their eldest daughter whom they had given up. When Carrie, the daughter, was eighteen she met her real parents who were overcome with joy. They introduced her to her siblings, full siblings, and tried to draw her into their family's life. Carrie rejected them, resenting their over-enthusiastic efforts to assimilate her. Her family, she told me, was her adoptive parents. They are Mom and Dad, not the birth parents.

There are no conclusions from any of this. Some families work, others don't. Carrie's adoption was a success, mine was a failure. The tragedy of mine was not my tragedy, but Joseph and Marjorie's. To adopt a child is an act of generosity, and they gave to me liberally, and in the end were bitterly disappointed in me. But my job was not to make them happy, but to survive, and survival meant rejecting them, their ways and even their name. After Joseph died I legally changed my name back to Cornwell, the last step of rejection and a symbol of conversion, because I am, at last, converted. I am H - A -P - P - Y, but my conversion was to atheism and frivolity. I recall a Peculiar People chapel, bare and cold, its sole decoration a scroll painted above the preacher's dais on which, in letters of red and gold, was written 'Be Sure Your Sin Will Find You Out'. In Cape Cod, on a beam above my desk, I have painted in letters of red and gold my favorite Shakespeare quotation; 'Dost thou think, because thou art virtuous, there shall be no more cakes and ale?'

THE SHARPE BOOKS

(in chronological order)

SHARPE'S TIGER
Richard Sharpe and the Siege of Seringapatam
1977

SHARPE'S TRIUMPH
Richard Sharpe and the Battle of Assaye
September 1803

SHARPE'S FORTRESS
Richard Sharpe and the Siege of Gawilghur
December 1803

SHARPE'S TRAFALGAR
Richard Sharpe and the Battle of Trafalgar
21 October 1805

SHARPE'S PREY
Richard Sharpe and the Expedition to Copenhagen
1807

SHARPE'S RIFLES
Richard Sharpe and the French Invasion of Galicia
January 1809

SHARPE'S HAVOC
Richard Sharpe and the Campaign in Northern Portugal
Spring 1809

SHARPE'S EAGLE
Richard Sharpe and the Talavera Campaign
July 1809

SHARPE'S GOLD
Richard Sharpe and the Destruction of Almeida
August 1810

SHARPE'S ESCAPE
Richard Sharpe and the Bussaco Campaign
1810

SHARPE'S FURY
Richard Sharpe and the Battle of Barrosa
March 1811

SHARPE'S BATTLE
Richard Sharpe and the Battle of Fuentes de Oñoro
May 1811

SHARPE'S COMPANY
Richard Sharpe and the Siege of Badajoz
January to April 1812

SHARPE'S SWORD
Richard Sharpe and the Salamanca Campaign
June and July 1812

SHARPE'S ENEMY
Richard Sharpe and the Defence of Portugal
Christmas 1812

SHARPE'S HONOUR
Richard Sharpe and the Vitoria Campaign
February to June 1813

SHARPE'S REGIMENT
Richard Sharpe and the Invasion of France
June to November 1813

SHARPE'S SIEGE
Richard Sharpe and the Winter Campaign
1814

SHARPE'S REVENGE
Richard Sharpe and the Peace of 1814

SHARPE'S WATERLOO
Richard Sharpe and the Waterloo Campaign
15 June to 18 June 1815

SHARPE'S DEVIL
Richard Sharpe and the Emperor
1820-21

SHARPE SHORT STORIES

SHARPE'S SKIRMISH
Summer 1812

SHARPE'S CHRISTMAS
Christmas 1813

SHARPE'S RANSOM
Christmas 1816

OTHER BOOKS

by

BERNARD CORNWELL

THE LAST KINGDOM
THE PALE HORSEMAN
LORDS OF THE NORTH
SWORD SONG

THE WINTER KING
ENEMY OF GOD
EXCALIBUR

HARLEQUIN
VAGABOND
HERETIC

REBEL
COPPERHEAD
BATTLE FLAG
THE BLOODY GROUND

WILDTRACK
SEALORD
CRACKDOWN
STORMCHILD
SCOUNDREL

STONEHENGE

REDCOAT

GALLOWS THIEF

A CROWNING MERCY
FALLEN ANGELS

www.bernardcornwell.net